j946   Shubert, Adrian, C.2
S   1953-

         The land and people
         of Spain.

$17.89

DATE		
JUL 0 1 1993		
NOV 1 8 1993		
NOV 0 4 1994 Pg		
APR 3 0 1996		
APR 1 0 1997		
APR 0 9 1998		

The Land and People of

SPAIN

Published Portraits of the Nations books

The Land and People of ®
SPAIN

by Adrian Shubert

HarperCollins*Publishers*

For Esther

Country maps by Robert Romagnoli
Photo research by Rod Beebe
Every effort has been made to locate the copyright holders of all copyrighted
materials and to secure from them the necessary publication permissions. In the
event that any questions arise with regard to the use of copyrighted materials, the
publisher will be glad to make necessary changes in future printings and editions.
Sources and credits for extracts appear on pages 234–237. All unaccredited translations from Spanish and Catalan are by the author.

THE LAND AND PEOPLE OF
is a registered trademark of
HarperCollins Publishers.

The Land and People of Spain
Copyright © 1992 by HarperCollins Publishers
Printed in the U.S.A. All rights reserved.
For information address HarperCollins Children's Books,
a division of HarperCollins Publishers,
10 East 53rd Street, New York, NY 10022.

Library of Congress Cataloging-in-Publication Data
Shubert, Adrian, date
    The land and people of Spain / by Adrian Shubert.
        p.   cm.   —   (Portraits of the nations)
    Includes bibliographical references and index.
    Filmography:
    Discography:
    Summary: Introduces the history, geography, people, culture, gov-
ernment, and economy of Spain.
    ISBN 0-06-020217-3. — ISBN 0-06-020218-1 (lib. bdg.)
    1. Spain—Juvenile literature. [1. Spain.] I. Title.
II. Series.
DP17.S48   1992   91-9971
946—dc20   CIP
                                                       AC

1 2 3 4 5 6 7 8 9 10
First Edition

Contents

Mini Facts

OFFICIAL NAME: Spain (España)

LOCATION: Bounded on the north by France, the Pyrenees, and the Bay of Biscay and the Atlantic Ocean; on the south by the Mediterranean Sea and the Straits of Gibraltar; on the east by the Mediterranean; and on the west by Portugal and the Atlantic Ocean.

AREA: 194,884 square miles (504,750 square kilometers)

CAPITAL: Madrid

POPULATION: 39,623,000 (1990 estimated)

MAJOR LANGUAGES: Spanish—also known as Castilian, the official state language; Gallego; Catalan; Basque

RELIGIONS: There is no official religion. The religion of the vast majority is Roman Catholicism. There are approximately 250,000 other Christians, 200,000 to 300,000 Moslems, and 13,000 Jews.

TYPE OF GOVERNMENT: Constitutional Monarchy

HEAD OF STATE: King Juan Carlos I

HEAD OF GOVERNMENT: President

PARLIAMENT: Congress of Deputies—350 members elected for 4-year terms
Senate—208 members elected for 4-year terms

ADMINISTRATIVE SUBDIVISIONS: 17 autonomous regions
50 provinces plus two municipalities in northern Morocco

ADULT LITERACY: 97 percent (1989)

LIFE EXPECTANCY: Female, 80; male, 74 (1989)

MAIN PRODUCTS: *Agriculture*—wine, citrus fruits, barley
Industry—automobiles, textiles, shoes

GROSS NATIONAL PRODUCT PER CAPITA: $7,740 (1988)

CURRENCY: Peseta; $1=107 pesetas (October, 1991)

THE WORLD

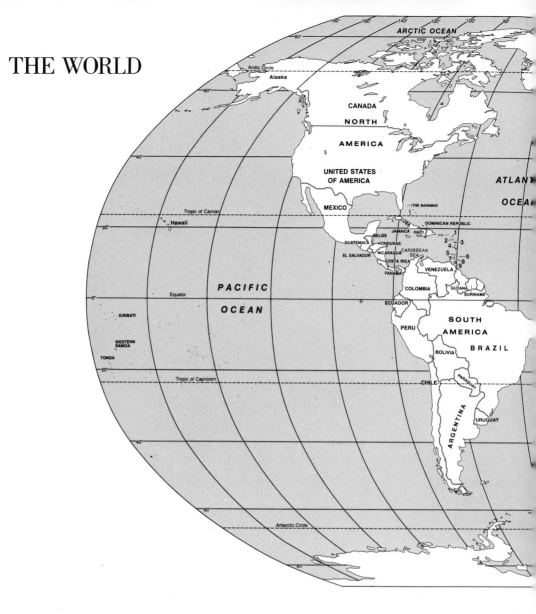

This world map is based on a projection developed by Arthur H. Robinson. The shape of each country and its size, relative to other countries, are more accurately expressed here than in previous maps. The map also gives equal importance to all of the continents, instead of placing North America at the center of the world. *Used by permission of the Foreign Policy Association.*

Legend

—— International boundaries

------- Disputed or undefined boundaries

Projection: Robinson

| 0 | 1000 | 2000 | 3000 Miles |
| 0 | 1000 | 2000 | 3000 Kilometers |

Caribbean Nations

1. Anguilla
2. St. Christopher and Nevis
3. Antigua and Barbuda
4. Dominica
5. St. Lucia
6. Barbados
7. St. Vincent
8. Grenada
9. Trinidad and Tobago

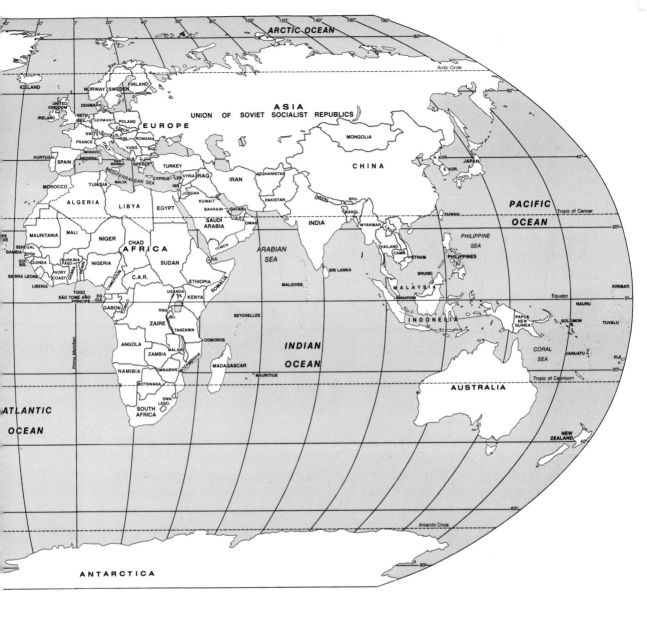

Abbreviations

ALB.	—Albania	C.A.R.	—Central African Republic	LEB.	—Lebanon	SWA.	—Swaziland
AUS.	—Austria	CZECH.	—Czechoslovakia	LESO.	—Lesotho	SWITZ.	—Switzerland
BANGL.	—Bangladesh	DJI.	—Djibouti	LIE.	—Liechtenstein	U.A.E.	—United Arab Emirates
BEL.	—Belgium	EQ. GUI.	—Equatorial Guinea	LUX.	—Luxemburg	YUGO.	—Yugoslavia
BHU.	—Bhutan	GER.	Germany	NETH.	—Netherlands		
BU.	—Burundi	GUI. BIS.	—Guinea Bissau	N. KOR.	—North Korea		
BUL.	—Bulgaria	HUN.	—Hungary	RWA.	—Rwanda		
CAMB.	—Cambodia	ISR.	—Israel	S. KOR.	—South Korea		

Questions
of Identity

Should the conquest of America be stopped? Did the king of Spain have the right to declare war on the Indians of America before they had been brought the word of God? From mid-August to mid-September 1550 a tribunal of theologians and government officials handpicked by Charles V of Spain, the mightiest ruler of the day, listened as two monks argued over the fate of the people of an entire hemisphere.

The sixty-year-old scholar Juan Ginés de Sepúlveda defended the right of Spain to wage war on a people whom he called natural slaves. His opponent, Bartolomé de Las Casas, argued that the conquest of the natives of America was not at all just and that if they were to be converted to Christianity, it had to be by peaceful means alone.

Las Casas was also a monk, but one with a most unusual background. Born in Seville in 1474, he went to America as a conquistador in 1502, only a decade after Columbus had arrived there. But he soon became convinced of the injustice of the conquest, and at the age of forty he gave up his estates and his Indians and joined the Dominican order. He devoted the rest of his long life to defending the Indians from his fellow Spaniards.

His success was limited. Attempts to set up special colonies for the Indians failed, and they continued to be forced to labor for their Spanish masters. The great debate of 1550 was also inconclusive. Both Sepúlveda and Las Casas claimed victory but the court never issued a verdict. The conquest of America, and its peoples, continued.

Las Casas made his strongest defense of the Indians in a book, *Very Brief Account of the Destruction of the Indies*,* published in 1552. Soon translated into English, Dutch, and many other languages under lurid titles and well stocked with grotesque illustrations, the book was republished many times. Here are some titles given to English translations of Las Casas:

1583	*The Spanish Colonie; or Briefe chronicle of the acts and gestes of the Spaniardes in the West Indies, called the newe world*
1626	*A Historical and True Account of the Cruel Massacre and Slaughter of 20,000,000 of people in the West Indies by the Spaniards*
1656	*The Tears of the Indians, being an historical account of the cruel massacres and slaughters of above twenty millions of innocent people, committed by the Spaniards*

*Throughout this book, the titles of foreign language works are given in English, unless they are generally known by their original titles.

· 2 ·

1689	*Popery Truly Displayed in its Bloody Colours;*
	or a Faithful Narrative of the Horrid and
	Unexampled Massacres, Butcheries and all
	manner of Cruelties that Hell and Malice could
	invent, committed by the Popish Spanish Party
	on the Inhabitants of West India
1699	*A Relation of the first voyages and*
	discoveries made by the Spanish in America.
	With an account of their unparalleled
	cruelties on the Indians, in the destruction
	of above 40 millions of people

Why was Las Casas' book so popular? To defend the Indians Las Casas had to attack the behavior of the Spanish, and he did so with great vigor. People in other countries were interested, but not because they cared for the Indians: They wanted horror stories about the Spaniards.

In the sixteenth century Spain was the greatest power in Europe and the center of a truly worldwide empire. Spain was also the leading Catholic state and, under Charles V and Philip II, one dedicated to defending Catholicism from newly emergent Protestantism. For the Protestants, and especially for the English and the Dutch, Spain was the great enemy, the evil empire of the day.

Las Casas' denunciation of the Spaniards in America was written to convince his compatriots to change their behavior. The book also made ideal propaganda for countries engaged in struggles with Spain. It became the most important basis of the Black Legend, the stereotype of Spaniards as a bloodthirsty, bigoted, corrupt, and authoritarian people. To exaggerated tales of the treatment of the Indians were added fanciful accounts of the horrors of the Spanish Inquisition and the brutality

SPAIN
PROVINCES AND PROVINCIAL CAPITALS
Names of provinces are in capital letters.
Except as noted, provincial capitals bear the name
of the province of which they are a part.

km	0	80	160	240	320
miles	0	50	100	150	200

FRANCE

ANDORRA

ÁLAVA
Vitoria

SANTANDER

VIZCAYA
Bilbao

GUIPÚZCOA
San Sebastián

LA CORUÑA

OVIEDO

LUGO

LEÓN

PALENCIA

BURGOS

Pamplona

NAVARRE

HUESCA

GERONA

LÉRIDA

PONTEVEDRA

ORENSE

LOGROÑO

ZAMORA

VALLA-
DOLID

SORIA

ZARAGOZA

BARCELONA

TARRAGONA

SEGOVIA

SALAMANCA

ÁVILA

MADRID

GUADALAJARA

TERUEL

CASTELLÓN

PORTUGAL

CÁCERES

TOLEDO

CUENCA

VALENCIA

Minorca

Majorca
Palma

Ibiza

BALEARIC
ISLANDS

Formentera

BADAJOZ

CIUDAD REAL

ALBACETE

ALICANTE

Mediterranean
Sea

CÓRDOBA

JAÉN

MURCIA

HUELVA

SEVILLE

GRANADA

ALMERÍA

Atlantic
Ocean

MÁLAGA

CÁDIZ

Strait of Gibraltar

Ceuta (Spain)

Melilla
(Spain)

AFRICA

CANARY ISLANDS
(Spain)

La Palma

Tenerife

Lanzarote

Las
Palmas

Gomera

Fuerteventura

Hierro

Gran Canaria

SPAIN

PORTUGAL

The Black Legend

From the first English translation of Las Casas (1583):

The Spaniards with their horses, their spears and their lances began to commit murders and strange cruelties. They entered into Towns, Boroughs and Villages, sparing neither women with child, neither them that layed in, but that they ripped their bellies, cut them in pieces, as if they had been opening of lambs shut up in their fold. They layed wagers [with dares to see who could] with one thrust of a sword paunch or bowel a man, cut off his head, or would best pierce his entrails at one stroke.

J. J. Ingalls, *America's War for Humanity* (1898):

Spain has been tried and convicted in the forum of history. Her religion has been bigotry, whose sacraments have been solemnized by the faggot and the rack. Her statesmanship has been infamy; her diplomacy hypocrisy; her wars have been massacres; her supremacy has been a blight and a curse, condemning continents to sterility and their inhabitants to death.

perpetrated by the Spaniards upon the Dutch in their war of independence.

The Black Legend has had a long life. As late as 1898 a new version of Las Casas' book was published in New York to help justify the Spanish-American War, and other works of pro-American propaganda carried the same message.

The Black Legend contains much exaggeration but it is not a total invention. The Spaniards' conquest of America was brutal, and so was much of their treatment of the Indians. But the Black Legend painted the Spaniards as vastly more brutal than other Europeans, and this is certainly questionable. In the parts of the New World that the French and English came to control, they too were responsible for the destruction of Indian civilizations. So, when their turn came, were the Americans. More indigenous people died as a result of the Spanish conquest—perhaps as many as 25 million in a century in Mexico alone—but most fell victim to European diseases against which their bodies had no defenses. In any case, would comparing such numbers tell us if one set of Europeans was better or worse than the other?

Romantic Spain

In the nineteenth century the Black Legend was overtaken by another stereotype, that of "romantic" Spain. Other Europeans, and above all the French, discovered in Spain a backward but exotic land full of colorful, violent, and passionate people. Spain became fashionable, and many foreign artists created works with Spanish settings and Spanish themes. These are some famous nineteenth-century works of literature and music by non-Spaniards with Spanish themes:

Literature
    Washington Irving, *The Alhambra*, 1832
    Victor Hugo, *Hernani*, 1830; *Ruy Blas*, 1838
    Prosper Mérimée, *Carmen*, 1845
    Théophile Gautier, *Wanderings in Spain*, 1845
Music
    Gioacchino Rossini, *The Barber of Seville*, 1816
    Felix Mendelssohn, *Ruy Blas*, 1839
    Giuseppe Verdi, *Ernani*, 1844; *Don Carlos*, 1867

Édouard Lalo, *Symphonie Espagnole*, 1874
Georges Bizet, *Carmen*, 1875
Jules Massenet, *Le Cid*, 1885

Most of these foreigners drew their inspiration from a single part of Spain, the south. There they were attracted to those features that were least like their own countries, such as the heritage of the Arabs and the presence of Gypsies and their art forms, such as flamenco. Foreigners were much less interested in mundane reality, such as the cotton mills of Barcelona or the coal mines of Asturias. The picture they left could only be distorted, but their genius made it a powerful and enduring one. How many people have taken their idea of what the Spaniards are like from Bizet's *Carmen*, the most popular opera of all time? And when we hear the word Spain, how many of us immediately think of the energy of flamenco and the bravery of the bullfighter?

Bullfight

The bullfight provides a link between the Black Legend and the romantic view of Spain. It also pulls foreigners in two directions. The matador is a glamorous and heroic figure, but the spectacle seems a cruel and barbaric one that could only be enjoyed by a cruel and barbaric people. Where else do thousands of people pay to watch men confront and kill savage animals? Where else do the men who do it become national heroes, and millionaires?

These stereotypes, the Black Legend and romantic Spain, have long misled foreigners about who the Spaniards really are. To be fair, even the Spaniards themselves have not been clear about their own identity.

Their confusion has centered on the question of whether the Spanish identity is based on uniformity or diversity. Do all Spaniards share a

Palaces and Gypsies

Washington Irving takes up residence at the Alhambra, Granada, 1829:

Here then I am, nestled in one of the most remarkable, romantic and delicious spots in the world. I have the complete range and I may say control of the whole palace. . . . I breakfast in the saloon of the ambassadors, or among the flowers and fountains in the Court of the Lions, and when I am not occupied with my pen, I lounge with my book about these oriental apartments or stroll about the courts and gardens and arcades by day or night with no one to interrupt me. It absolutely appears to me like a dream; or as if I am spellbound in some fairy palace.

Mérimée introduces "Carmen":

I very much doubted whether the Señorita Carmen was a pureblooded gypsy. At all events she was infinitely prettier than any other woman of her race I have ever seen. . . . There was something strange and wild about her beauty. . . . Her eyes, especially, had an expression of mingled sensuality and fierceness which I had never seen in any other human glance.

A gypsy caravan on the road in southern Spain, 1985. Gypsies were central to the nineteenth-century image of Spain as an exotic country. Roseanne Lufrano

Two Tourists Go to the Bullfight

Harry A. Franck (1926):

There is an intensity in the moment of a matador standing with steeled eyes and bared sword before a bull panting in tired anger, head lowered, a hush of expectancy in the vast audience, the [assistants] poised on tiptoes at a little distance, an equine corpse or two tumbled on the sand to give the scene reality, compared with which the third man, third strike in the ninth inning of a 0–0 contest is as exciting as a game of marbles.

G. W. Thornbury (1859):

. . . It inures the mind to the sight of blood and hardens the heart. No wonder the Spaniard is too fond of using his knife; no wonder he thinks [nothing] of taking life when he can do it safely. . . . All we can say for it is that it must be tolerated in a nation who, neither sensitive or thoughtful, are at least two centuries behind ourselves. We once had our bull-baitings; we once used the knife as freely as the Spaniard. The coarser nerved Spaniard, in seeing the bullfight, sees a habitual thing and has not the sense of sharing in a crime that we have.

Moments from a bullfight. Leading bullfighters are idolized and make huge sums of money.   Paul A. McDonough

single heritage or are they really a mix of very distinct peoples? That the question was ever asked seems surprising. Diversity is inescapable in Spanish history. What we now call Spain grew out of the union in the fifteenth century of two separate states, Castile and Aragon; but regional identities persisted and in the nineteenth century spawned movements for home rule or regional autonomy. Castilian, generally known as Spanish, has been the language of the state, but at least three other languages have always been quite widely spoken and at times have had literary traditions.

The Languages of Spain

Four languages are currently spoken in Spain. The official language of the state is Castilian, *castellano*, which foreigners generally call Spanish. Each of the other languages has official status in one of the country's autonomous regions: Catalan in Catalonia, Basque (Euskera) in Euzkadi (the Basque Provinces), and Gallego in Galicia.

Castilian, Catalan, and Gallego are all Romance languages—that is, they all evolved out of Latin. Gallego is closely related to Portuguese, from which it separated only in the fourteenth century. It was the language of courtly literature until the beginning of the fifteenth century, when it ceased to be used in literature or for official purposes and became limited to everyday use. A literary revival began in the nineteenth century, and since the 1970's Gallego has reemerged as a serious literary language.

Catalan shares many similarities with Provençal of southern France. It flourished as a language of literature and scholarship in the medieval period but declined after the fifteenth century. In the nineteenth century it enjoyed a revival as a literary language in the movement known as the Renaixença.

Castilian began as a dialect spoken in northernmost Spain. In the twelfth century it became the language of the court of the monarchy of Castile and began to emerge as a literary language. The political dominance of Castile from the sixteenth century on allowed Castilian to become the dominant language and ultimately the official language of the Spanish state.

Euskera is totally unrelated to the Romance family of languages, or to any other known language, and it is something of a mystery language. The origins of Euskera are unclear, although scholars have suggested that it might have come from North Africa or the Caucasus, or that it is distantly related to Finnish or Magyar. Until the end of the nineteenth century Euskera was the language of the Basque countryside. It was not much spoken in the towns and it had no literary tradition. In the twentieth century, and especially since 1975, Euskera has become more widely spoken and has begun to be used in literature, journalism, and the movies, and on television.

Convivencia

In the Middle Ages Spain was the great cultural crossroads of Europe, a home to Christians, Moslems, and Jews. There was conflict among them but also *convivencia*—cooperation and cross-fertilization that produced cultures of real brilliance.

Despite this evidence of diversity, since the end of the fifteenth century Spaniards have repeatedly rejected much of their heritage and sought their national identity in uniformity. From this point of view being Spanish meant speaking Castilian and being Catholic.

The meaning of Spanish history was the center of a debate in the 1950's and 1960's between two of Spain's greatest intellectuals. Americo Castro argued that the Spanish identity has diverse roots:

The Spanish people came into being as a conglomeration of three castes of believers—Christians, Moors and Jews.

From the struggles and rivalries among these three groups, from their inter-connection and their hatred, arose the authentic life of the Spaniards. . . . The life that is now Spanish was a fabric woven of three threads, none of which may be cut out.

Claudio Sánchez Albornoz violently disagreed. As he saw it the Spanish identity was Catholic, forged out of the struggle against other peoples in the peninsula.

Symbiosis and co-existence? An absurd theory. [It was] a ferocious, centuries long struggle of the Christians against the two enemies, against the Moors with whom they were in a life and death struggle . . . and against the Jews who had exploited them and continued exploiting them . . .

The struggle against the Moors created the men who made Spain and the Spanishness of the new times. . . . The war against the Moor and the fight against the Jew affirmed and exalted the old temperament of *homo hispanus,* whose body was prepared for abstinence and fatigue and whose soul was pre-pared for death and who experienced his relations with God in a special way. . . .

The Catholic kings used the Inquisition to affirm the religious unity of their subjects, the unity for which Spanish Christians had fought for nearly eight centuries. . . . One door in Spanish history closed and Spain truly came into existence.

The disputes over such questions have usually engaged scholars, but they have not always been limited to them or taken place only on pa-per. At times political conflicts have been expressed in terms of the meaning of being Spanish. And once, from 1936 to 1939, a civil war was fought between the defenders of a unified Catholic Spain and the advocates of a more pluralistic vision of the country.

Who are the Spaniards then? What, if anything, does it mean to be Spanish? How have they been able to answer these questions for them-selves? Do such questions even have answers?

The Land

Spain lies at the western extreme of the European continent, sharing the Iberian peninsula with its neighbor Portugal. The nation covers an area of 194,884 square miles (504,750 square kilometers), a territory slightly smaller than that of France. This makes it a large country by European standards, although a North American would not be too impressed. Spain could fit easily into the state of Texas, and three times into Alaska. At its widest point it extends 600 miles (970 kilometers) from north to south and 660 miles (1,060 kilometers) from east to west, about the distance between Kansas City and Denver or Atlanta and Washington, D.C.

Much of the western boundary is formed by the border with Portugal, and to the northeast the Pyrenees separate Spain from France. On the other sides it is bounded by water: the Mediterranean Sea to the east and south, the Bay of Biscay and the Atlantic Ocean to the north.

Spain is the most mountainous country in Europe after Switzerland. Here the village of Potes, in the province of Santander, lies in the shadow of the Picos de Europa range.
Courtesy of the Tourist Office of Spain

Spain has 2,340 miles (3,765 kilometers) of coastline.

Two sets of islands, the Balearics in the Mediterranean and the Canaries in the Atlantic, also form part of the country. So do Ceuta and Melilla, two enclaves on the coast of North Africa.

Mountains

The physical environments of Spain are many and varied. The most striking feature is the prevalence of mountains. After Switzerland, Spain is the most mountainous country in Europe. The Pyrenees, at a constant height of at least 5,000 feet (1,500 meters) and rising above 11,000 feet (3,300 meters) in places, block the northern overland entrance to the Iberian peninsula. The Cantabrian range, which averages between 5,000 and 6,000 feet (1,500 and 1,800 meters), cuts the northern tier—Galicia, Asturias, Santander, and the Basque country—from the rest of the country. After a narrow valley the Iberian Mountains begin, running roughly parallel to the Pyrenees. The vast central *meseta*, or tableland, is broken into two by the central sierras,

PHYSICAL FEATURES

Elevation above sea level:

over 3000 feet

over 1500 feet

FRANCE

ANDORRA

PYRENEES

Llobregat River

Ebro River

Mediterranean Sea

Bay of Biscay

CANTABRIAN MTS

Esla River

Duero River

IBERIAN MTS

SIERRA DE GUADARRAMA

CENTRAL SIERRA

SIERRA DE GREDOS

Tagus River

Guadiana River

SIERRA MORENA

Guadalquivir River

BETIC CORDILLERA

SIERRA NEVADA

Mulhacén

PORTUGAL

Atlantic Ocean

or mountain ranges, the Gredos and the Guadarrama. In the south the Betic Cordillera, an irregular series of mountain ridges broken by north-south rifts, contains the mainland's tallest peak, Mulhacén, at 11,407 feet (3,476 meters). The highest point in all of Spain is the Pico de Teide, in the Canary Islands, which rises 12,178 feet (3,712 meters).

The *Meseta*

After the mountains, the country is dominated by the high plateau of the *meseta*. The northern *meseta* covers some 15,000 square miles (38,800 square kilometers) and has an average altitude of 2,700 feet (820 meters). The southern *meseta* is three times as large but has a lower average elevation, less than 2,000 feet (600 meters). The coastal lowlands are very small. Catalonia, for example, has a very narrow coastal strip, which is brought to an abrupt end by mountains only twelve miles inland. Rose Macaulay, an Englishwoman who drove through Spain in 1949, described the coastal highway there:

The road, the old Roman road from Gaul to Tarragona, sweeps up from [the French border] in wild and noble curves, lying like a curled snake along the barren mountain flanks of the Alta Ampurdán, climbing dizzily up, darting steeply down into gorges and ravines, above deep rocky inlets where blue water thrusts into rock-bound coves. . . . Points and capes jut boldly through thin blue air above a deep cobalt sea; rocky islets lie offshore; the road dips down to the little bay of Culera. . . . Above it on both sides of the bay tower great bare mountains, their faint evanescent colours shifting with each turn of light and shadow.

The great tableland is flat, but forbidding. There are few trees, only clumps of *encinas*, a kind of dwarf oak. Most of what Castilians call rivers would seem creeks to North American eyes. The land is not particularly fertile, and rainfall is irregular. The tableland can seem a sad and forbidding place. Antonio Machado captured this sensation in his poem "Banks of the Duero," written early in the twentieth century:

> I saw the horizon enclosed by dark knolls
> and rimmed with northern and evergreen oaks;
> denuded cliffsides and a humble green
> where the merinos graze and the bull on its knees
> broods in the grass; the borders of the river
> where clear summer sun lights the green poplars;
> and silently, some distant travellers,
> so minute!—carts, riders and muleteers—
> cross the long bridge, and below the arcades
> of stone, waters of the Duero in dark shades
> of silver.
>   The Duero crosses the oaken heart
> of Iberia and Castile.
>   O land apart
> sad and noble; high plains, wastelands and stone,
> terrain without plow or streams, treeless zones,
> decrepit cities, roads without inns, and throngs
> of stupefied peasants, without dance or song,
> who from dying hearths still break free,
> like your long rivers, Castile, toward the sea! . . .
> The sun is setting. From the distant town
> I hear the pulsing bells resound:
> old women in mourning go to intone
> their Rosary. Two weasels slip between big stones,
> see me, run off, and gaping, reappear.
> The fields are fading on the sombre sphere.
> Along the white road an inn, open, alone,
> faces the dark fields and a desert of stone.

Rivers

The mountains make movement from one region to another difficult and obstruct movement even within individual regions, such as the Ebro basin and the Cantabrian strip. The principal rivers are the Tagus (626 miles; 1,007 kilometers), the Ebro (565 miles; 909 kilometers), the Duero (525 miles; 845 kilometers), the Guadiana (515 miles; 829 kilometers) and the Guadalquivir (408 miles; 656 kilometers). Unfortunately, they are too fast-flowing or suffer too much silting at their mouths to serve as aids to communication and transportation. Only the construction of a nationwide railway system after 1850 made it possible to move easily from one region to another.

Dreary Wastes

Spanish railways are notoriously bad, but before they were built traveling was hard and unpleasant. George Ticknor, who became the founder of Hispanic studies in the United States, traveled through Spain in 1818 and found the twelve-day trip from Barcelona to Madrid one of the worst of his wide experience:

A lone dwarf oak stands out in the vast Castilian tableland.   Angel Esteban Martín

Excepting Daroca, we passed for six days through no place that deserved to be called a town. . . . All the rest of the way was through dreary wastes where the guidebook coolly and laconically informs you from time to time there is danger of robbery; and if perchance there was a village, it was too squalid, miserable and poor to afford anything but bread and wine. . . . From Barcelona to Madrid I did not once sleep upon a bed, and several times merely rolled myself up in my great coat and lay down on the floor, which was badly paved. Twice I dined in the same apartment with our mules, who were not two steps from me.

Climate

Spain also has a tremendously wide range of climates, from temperate in the northwest to semiarid in the south. Some areas in the northwest get between 60 and 70 inches (150 and 180 centimeters) of rain per year, but some two thirds of the country is deficient in rainfall—that is, it does not get enough rain to sustain normal plant growth—four months out of twelve.

There are three main climatic zones. The maritime zone, extending from the north coast to the Cantabrian mountains, includes Galicia, Asturias, Santander, and the Basque Provinces and has mild winters, abundant precipitation spread throughout the year, and warm, but not hot, summers.

The inland areas—the *mesetas*, the Ebro basin, and the adjoining mountains—have a continental climate, as in Montana. Temperatures fluctuate greatly, both from winter to summer and from day to night. The summers are very hot and the winters very cold. In January the average temperature in many parts of the northern *meseta* is only a couple of degrees above freezing. Spaniards have a saying about the climate here: *Nueve meses de invierno y tres meses de infierno*—nine months of winter and three months of hell. Rainfall is low and irregular throughout the year. (That most famous weather report "The rain in Spain falls mainly on the plain" is utterly misleading.)

The final climate is the Mediterranean zone, which takes in the Andalusian plain and the southern and eastern coastal strips. There is little variation in temperature from winter to summer, and in both seasons temperatures are higher than in the interior. The hottest area is between Seville and Córdoba, where the mean temperature in July and August is between 85° and 88° Fahrenheit (29° and 31° Celsius) and readings of more than 100° Fahrenheit (38° Celsius) are common.

Geography, Landscape, and Environment

A country's basic geography changes very slowly, if at all. Landscapes and environment, what human beings do with the geography they inherit, are much shorter-lived. Through the economic activities they undertake, men and women can change the face of a country very quickly. Woodlands disappear as the frontiers of cultivation expand, wildlife is killed off, rivers are polluted. These changes, especially those associated with industrialization, are often ecologically harmful, but they are also indicators of expanding industry and a growing population.

Changing landscapes and environmental degradation came quickly to the Asturias, a region of north-central Spain which became the center of the country's coal-mining industry. Before mining got underway on a large scale, this mountainous area was a place of dramatic beauty. In the 1780's a British traveler wrote that "instead of soft and swelling

Wet Spain/Dry Spain

These differences in geography and climate dictate differences in agriculture. In the north and northwest, frequently known as "wet Spain," the dominant cereal crop is corn. The heavy rainfall and the relatively low summer temperatures mean that most of this region does not produce grapes or, therefore, wine. The inland areas of Galicia are the one exception. Cider, made from apples, is the usual substitute. Hazelnuts are another major crop.

Grapevines are found in many other places: in Catalonia, Valencia,

hills covered with grass or clothed with woods, scarcely anything was to be seen but stupendous rocks of limestone, some in long ridges rising perpendicular to the height of two or three hundred feet, others cragged and broken into a thousand forms." Fifty years later, a Spanish encyclopedia could say that "the mountains give way to a number of hills between which there are valleys which are extensive and very attractive. On the slopes are beautiful fields and meadows."

By the 1860's things were very different. Slag heaps occupied more and more of the landscape. The rivers, which had been home to large stocks of salmon, were so polluted that people complained to local government that "we cannot wash our clothes or cook or even let the cattle drink." Population grew and cities emerged, but there was no sewage disposal beyond discharging it straight into the rivers. By the 1880's, infectious diseases, such as cholera and typhus, became increasingly common.

The caves of Almanzora in the southern province of Almería. The terrain so resembles the southwestern United States that many western movies were made here in the 1960's and 1970's.   Courtesy of the Tourist Office of Spain

Aragon, Castile, and Andalusia. Most of these grapes are used for producing wine. The best known and most prestigious wines are sherry, a fortified wine produced in a small area around Jerez de la Frontera in the province of Cádiz; the hearty reds of the Rioja, in the province of Logroño; and the whites of the Duero valley, especially from the province of Valladolid.

The area around Valencia, on the Mediterranean coast, is the one part of the country that is intensively irrigated. This allows the region to produce rice, which is the basis of Valencia's—and perhaps Spain's—most famous dish, paella. This region also produces large crops of vegetables and citrus fruits, especially oranges.

On the *meseta* and in the south, in "dry Spain," wheat, which requires less water, is the principal grain crop. Olive trees, which need long summers and little rain and can survive in thin, rocky soils, also cover much of this region.

Dry Spain, and particularly Andalusia, is the heartland of the

Spanish ranching industry. Open range ranching, of cattle and especially sheep, was probably "invented"—for Europe at least—in medieval Castile and spread south with the Reconquest. The economy of Andalusia, and of the Alentejo in Portugal, quickly came to be dominated by ranching. The Spaniards and Portuguese took their ranching economy, and methods such as the use of spurs, the roundup (rodeo), and branding, to the Americas.

This type of ranching also required the use of horses. Spain was the one part of medieval Europe where horses were abundant and within the means of many people, not just aristocrats. As a result, Spaniards became first-rate riders. The horses were also first-rate, a cross between the Iberian and Arabian breeds.

Ranchers in Salamanca in the 1970's. Ranching was an important part of the economy of medieval and early modern Spain. Spaniards took their techniques to the Americas.
Angel Esteban Martín

The sight of the southern countryside, with its mixture of wheat, olives, and livestock, was described by the American novelist William Dean Howells in *Familiar Spanish Travels*, a book based on his trip of 1911:

. . . The yellow Guadalquivir followed us all the way, in a valley that sometimes widened to the blue mountains always walling the horizon. . . . The olive orchards then seen afar were intimately realized more and more in their amazing extent. . . . They were regularly planted and most were in a vigorous middle life. . . . The orchards filled the level foregrounds and the hilly backgrounds to the vanishing-points of the mountainous perspectives; but when I say this I mean the reader to allow for wide expanses of pasturage, where lordly bulls were hoarding themselves for the feasts throughout Spain which the bulls of Andalusia are happy beyond others in supplying. With their devoted families they paraded the meadows, black against the green, or stood in sharp arrest, the most characteristic accent of the scene. In the farther rather than the nearer distance there were towns, very white, very African . . . beyond the wheatlands which disputed the landscape with the olive orchards. . . .

Settlement

The pattern of settlement in the countryside also varies significantly from region to region. In northern Spain population is dispersed, in numerous small hamlets and clusters of independent family farms known as *caseríos*. In the center, the typical pattern is one of villages whose population is made up overwhelmingly of farmers. In the south, where most people who work the land are wage laborers and not landowners or tenants, they live in agro-towns, urban centers of generally 5,000 to 10,000 people in which residents have a diverse mix of occupations.

Spaniards speak of various regional characters in their country, and these are often linked to climate and the physical environment. Castilians, faced with the tableland and an extreme climate, are said to be sad, sober, and long-suffering. Andalusians are considered hot-blooded and expressive, as well as untrustworthy. Galicians, who have to scratch a living out of tiny farms, are said to be especially careful with money. Catalonians are described as born business people. A pamphlet published in the middle of the nineteenth century listed the various regional characters in verse. Asturians, who come from a mountainous region famous for its wild boar and bear, were described—not entirely consistently—in this way:

The Asturian is like a pig,
Short, squat and stocky,
Tough, but deformed.
He is half man, half bear.
His character is honorable,
He is good, but innocent.
He does everything in a fury,
Is shallow and haughty,
And pretty lazy,
When it is time to work in the fields.

Resources

With such extensive coastlines, Spaniards almost inevitably became great fishermen. They have always heavily fished their own coastal waters, and they very quickly went farther afield. The most adventurous fishermen were those of the north coast, especially the Basques, who were among the first Europeans to exploit the Grand Banks, off eastern Canada. Spain still has one of the largest fishing fleets in the world, but Spanish fishermen now frequently come into conflict with the governments of other countries, such as Morocco and Canada, which have attempted to impose limits on the catches allowed to foreigners. Spaniards also fish their rivers. Some of the earliest known European treatises on fishing, from the sixteenth century, were written in Spain.

Spain has abundant mineral resources. In the nineteenth and early twentieth centuries it was the principal mining country in Europe, and minerals were one of the bases of the national economy. Iron ore from Vizcaya, copper from Río Tinto in Huelva, and mercury from Almadén in Ciudad Real were all major exports. Coal from Asturias helped power railroads and industry. Today the most important products are coal, zinc, lead, and copper, while bauxite, tin, tungsten, silver, manganese, and uranium are mined in smaller quantities.

Population

Spain's population is now 39 million. The population has grown rapidly in the twentieth century, and especially since 1940.

Unlike most other countries in western Europe, Spain has received virtually no immigrants. This means that almost all growth has been natural increase, that is, growth stemming from the difference between births and deaths.

This has happened even though the birth rate has fallen sharply, from 34.5 babies per 1,000 women of childbearing age per year in 1900 to only 13 in the mid-1980's. In 1982 the fertility rate dropped below replacement level—that is, Spanish women were not having enough babies to maintain the population at its current level. It has continued to drop since then.

But as the country became wealthier and a state health care system was created, the annual death rate fell even more quickly, from 28.8 deaths per 1,000 population in 1900 to 8.4 per 1,000 in 1970. The most dramatic change came in infant mortality, usually taken to be one of the best indicators of a country's level of development. Between

1960 and 1975 infant mortality was cut by 75 percent. (These changes also meant that Spaniards lived longer than before: average life expectancy is now 77 years, up from 35 at the beginning of the century.)

As it has grown, the distribution of the population has changed. These changes were underway in the nineteenth century but were most massive between 1950 and 1970. In 1940, more than a third of all Spaniards lived in towns with fewer than 5,000 people, but by 1970 only 22 percent did. In the process, many villages disappeared altogether: In 1984 one Spanish newspaper reported that there were 2,000 abandoned villages in the country. At the other end of the scale, the percentage of the population living in cities of more than half a million more than doubled, from 8.3 to 17.9 percent. By 1970 almost half, 49 percent, of all Spaniards lived in cities with more than 50,000 people; thirty years earlier only 24 percent had.

The port of Cedeira, in the province of La Coruña. Fishing has been, and remains, an important activity. Courtesy of the Tourist Office of Spain

Spaniards also use new methods of harvesting the seas. A lobster taken from a hatchery near Llanes, in Asturias.   Courtesy of the Tourist Office of Spain

At the same time, population shifted from some regions of the country to others. Areas that were industrializing gained, while those that were not lost. During the 1960's, twenty-three provinces lost population. The losses were heaviest in the two Castiles: Old Castile dropped from 2.85 million people in 1960 to 2.55 million in 1975; New Castile from 1.38 to 1.04 million. Five provinces—Ávila, Palencia, Segovia, Soria, and Zamora—had fewer people in 1975 than in 1900.

From the Iberians to the Visigoths

The remaining traces of the first human civilization in Spain are a number of impressive cave paintings, mostly of hunting scenes. The most famous and spectacular are at Altamira, in the northern province of Santander; these paintings date from around 12,000 B.C. Discovered in 1879, the Altamira depictions of bison, boar, wolf, and elk were so vivid that for more than twenty years scientists refused to accept them as authentic.

Spain first entered the written record in the Old Testament as Tarshish, a land of fabulous wealth, and throughout antiquity writers described it as an Eldorado, a land of gold. No wonder, then, that despite its position on the western edge of the Mediterranean world, Spain—or Iberia, as it was called—quickly and continually attracted the attention of the more advanced civilizations farther east. Beginning perhaps as early as 1100 B.C., outsiders, first the Phoenicians, then the Greeks and Carthaginians, set up trading posts and colonies on the southern and eastern coasts.

Traders and colonists who came to this rich land found a mosaic of peoples known collectively as the Iberians. These societies emerged before 2000 B.C., but archaeological evidence suggests that between 1200 and 1100 B.C. they experienced radical change in styles of housing and pottery, although the cause is not known. The Iberians had no central political authority. A monarchy, known as Tartessos, ruled much of the Guadalquivir valley, but the rest of Spain was divided into numerous city-states or, as in the interior and northwest, clans that would periodically join forces for military purposes. Warfare was common. There was no single Iberian culture or even a single language, although the languages of the Iberians were similar to each other.

Phoenicians and Greeks

The first outsiders to arrive from the east were the Phoenicians. Drawn by the mineral wealth of the kingdom of Tartessos, and especially the silver mines of Río Tinto, the Phoenicians established a series of colonies and trading posts along the southern coast. Soon members of the Iberian societies began to emulate the wealthier and more advanced Phoenicians, a development historians now call the "orientalizing period."

This was voluntary assimilation, not the product of imposition through conquest. It was also a process that was common throughout the Mediterranean basin. But not all members of Iberian society could take part. Usually only the rich and powerful, who controlled the gold and bronze the newcomers sought, could acquire new goods. These elites could afford to buy luxury items such as jewels, extravagant clothing, or weapons, which in turn allowed them to further assert their status and power. However, the Phoenicians also wanted products such as silver, salt, or dyes, which the Iberians had not valued, and this provided an opportunity for ambitious new traders to establish their fortunes.

The Greeks also came to Spain. Two colonies—Emporion, "the mar-

The Wealth of Iberia

Strabo was a Greek geographer and historian who was born in 63 B.C. His *Geography* is the first known attempt in the western world to bring together all geographical knowledge. Strabo did travel widely, although he did not visit all the places he described. The *Geography* consists of seventeen books, two of which deal with Spain:

Now, although [Spain] has been endowed with so many good things, still one might welcome and admire . . . most of all its natural richness in metals. For the whole country of the Iberians is full of metals, although not all of it is so rich in fruit, or so fertile either, and in particular that part which is well supplied with metals. It is rare for a country to be fortunate in both respects, and it is also rare for the same country to have within a small area an abundance of all kinds of metals. But there is no worthy word of praise left to him who wishes to praise their excellence in this respect. Up to the present moment in fact, neither gold, nor silver, nor yet copper, nor iron has been found anywhere in the world, in a natural state, either in such quantity or of such good quality.

The statue of an Iberian goddess known as the Lady of Elche.   Museo Arqueológico
Nacional, Madrid

ket," and Rode—were established around 575 B.C. While pottery from these settlements was traded all along the shores of the Mediterranean, the colonies did not expand beyond the northeast coast, in present-day Gerona.

The Great Power Struggle

In 573 B.C. the Phoenician city-states in what are now considered Israel and Lebanon were conquered by Babylon. This allowed Carthage, itself created as a Phoenician colony on the coast of North Africa, to become the dominant power in the western Mediterranean. For some 350 years the Carthaginians kept to the same area of coastline where the Phoenicians had operated and continued the same type of trade with the Iberians: exchanging luxury goods for silver, dyes, and olive oil.

This changed dramatically after 237 B.C. Driven by their defeat in the First Punic War with Rome, which deprived them of Sardinia and Sicily, the Carthaginians sought to expand their control in Spain. (See *The Land and People of Italy.*) Trade and peaceful cultural influence were no longer enough, and Carthage set out to conquer the peninsula. For the first time Spain found itself caught up in the struggles of distant great powers. Within less than twenty years Iberia would lose its independence to become part of an alien empire.

The Carthaginian conquest that began in 237 B.C. was led by three members of the Barca family: Hamilcar, Hasdrubal, and Hannibal. For the first time the Carthaginians moved beyond the coast, into the valley of the Guadalquivir. Both Hasdrubal and Hannibal used diplomatic as well as military means, marrying the daughters of Iberian rulers. Hannibal, who spent his career trying to defeat Rome and who was able to eventually lead his armies from Spain through France and into the heart of Italy, pushed into central Spain, as far north as Salamanca and perhaps the valley of the Ebro.

Hannibal's success caught the attention of the Romans, who feared that the Carthaginians might ally with the Gauls, in what is now France. Rome and Carthage signed a treaty in 225 B.C. in which the Carthaginians agreed to remain south of the Ebro. But when Hannibal sacked the city of Saguntum (present-day Sagunto), which had put itself under Roman protection, Rome declared war. This Second Punic War began in 218 B.C. By 206 B.C. the Romans had driven the Carthaginians from Spain, although the war would continue outside the peninsula for four more years.

The Romans did not have an easy time controlling the peninsula. Beginning in 206 B.C. they had to deal with recurrent revolts by tribes in various parts of Iberia. In 137 B.C. the Romans suffered one of the most humiliating defeats in their entire history, surrendering an army of twenty thousand men. Three years later Rome appointed Publius Cornelius Scipio Aemilianus, the general who had destroyed Carthage in 146 B.C., to direct the war in Spain. With sixty thousand men he laid siege to the stronghold of Numantia and eventually starved it into submission in 133 B.C. Some of the defenders preferred suicide to surrender, and this episode has been used since then as a symbol of the Spaniards' valor and love of liberty.

Roman Spain

The defeat of Numantia ended serious resistance to Roman rule in central Spain. Finally, after nearly one hundred years of continual warfare, Roman rule was secure.

Initially Roman Spain was divided into three provinces, but by the fourth century A.D. they had been increased to five: Tarraconensis, Carthaginensis, Baetica, Lusitania, and Gallaecia. Each province had a governor, appointed by Rome, who was responsible for military affairs and administration, especially the collection of revenue.

The Romans built an extensive network of roads to knit together the towns and forts. The towns were the centers of local government and of Roman culture. Some, the *colonaie*, were created by the Romans and populated with settlers from Italy, usually retired soldiers. The most spectacular of these settlements was Augusta Emerita, the capital of Lusitania, which was founded in 25 B.C. The model towns were intended to display the advantages of Roman life to the local elites.

The Romans also sponsored new native settlements and, beginning with Julius Caesar, granted the status of *municipium* to some of the more flourishing towns. The inhabitants of *municipia* received Latin status, an intermediate step on the way to Roman citizenship. Local magistrates could become Roman citizens after completing their term in office. Under the emperor Vespasian (ruled A.D. 69–79) all Spanish towns were given Latin status. In A.D. 212 the emperor Caracalla decreed that all the inhabitants of the empire could become citizens.

Cultural Assimilation

Rome imposed a single government on Spain but did not impose its culture on the natives. Instead, members of the local elite chose to adopt Roman ways in order to take advantage of the opportunities for participating in the public life of the empire. This process of cultural assimilation was not equally strong across Spain as a whole. It was much stronger in the south and east than in the northwest, where the Roman presence was smaller.

Religion   There was no uniformity even in the important realm of religion. Rome's religion, in which gods were imagined as people and represented by numerous statues, was alien to the Iberian tradition.

The Destruction of Numantia

The siege and destruction of Numantia by the Romans is an excellent example of how historical events can be used to create beliefs, or myths, about a people's history and character.

The events were described by Appian, a historian who wrote at some time between A.D. 50 and 150. His *Roman History* consisted of twenty-four volumes, written in Greek, that described numerous peoples, from the beginning of their known history until they were incorporated into the Roman Empire. Here is how he recounts the subjugation of Numantia:

> The Numantines, being oppressed by hunger, sent five men to Scipio to ask whether he would treat them with moderation if they would surrender. . . . Scipio . . . said merely that they must surrender their arms and place themselves and their city in his hands. . . .
>
> Soon after this, all their eatables being consumed, having neither flocks, nor grass, they began, as people are sometimes forced to do in war, to lick boiled hides. When these also failed they boiled and ate the bodies of human beings, first of those who had died a natural death, chopping them into small bits for cooking. Afterwards, being

Some of the Phoenician and Carthaginian deities became associated with Roman ones: The Phoenician Melkhaart became the Roman Hercules; the Carthaginian goddess Tanit became the Roman Juno. The Romans were generally tolerant of these other religions, which meant that some pre-Roman cults continued to survive, especially in the northern regions. It also meant that a number of new religions were imported from the eastern Mediterranean. The cults of Isis from Egypt

nauseated by the flesh of the sick, the stronger laid violent hands upon the weaker. . . . In this condition they surrendered themselves to Scipio. . . . But they put off the day [of surrender], declaring that many of them still clung to liberty and desired to take their own lives.

The sixteenth-century writer Miguel de Cervantes used the events as the basis of his verse play *The Siege of Numantia*, which closes with the following glorification of the defenders of Numantia, as foreshadowing the glories of the Spaniards of later centuries.

SCIPIO: O, never such a memorable event,
              Child of old and valiant heart
              Who, with this act brings glory
              Not only to Numantia but also to Spain.

FAME: Such a feat as this, never before seen,
              Shows the valor which, in coming centuries,
              Will have the heirs of such fathers,
              The sons of vigorous Spain.

and Mithras from Persia, which had stronger emotional and spiritual contents than the Roman beliefs, as well as a belief in rebirth and eternal life, found some followers in Iberia.

Most of these mystical religions required a series of costly initiation rites, which meant that they were open only to the elite. (This was not true of the most famous of all the eastern mystical religions, Christianity, which probably reached Spain in the second century A.D.) Aspiring members to the cult of Isis had to undergo ritual bathing, fasting, and contemplation before being accepted. In the second century A.D., one woman, Fabia Fabiana, celebrated joining the cult by dedicating a statue to the goddess as the protector of young girls and adorning it with precious stones.

Landowners and Slaves

Society in Roman Spain was hierarchical. At the bottom were the slaves, some of whom were able to buy their freedom. The slaves came from across the known world and from all ethnic groups. Above them were the freeborn, who ranged from farmers, fishermen, and construction workers to the wealthy elite who dominated local political life. The wealth of the elite was based on the ownership of large amounts of land, which they rented to tenants or worked with slave labor. Many landowners also became involved in lucrative commercial activities, such as the production and export of grain, wine, olive oil, and fish sauces. These people displayed their wealth by providing buildings such as baths, temples, and theaters for public use or sponsoring public banquets, chariot races, and gladiatorial combats.

A wealthy Iberian could also aspire to a role in the government of the empire, which was perhaps the most compelling reason for becoming a Roman. Those who owned property worth at least four hundred thousand sesterces could become knights and be named to military and administrative posts in the direct service of the emperor. (Four sesterces was the average daily wage for a worker.) Those who were worth 1 million sesterces could join the more prestigious senatorial order and might eventually become governors of provinces. By the first century A.D. several Spanish senatorial families became highly influential in Rome itself. Two even produced emperors: Trajan (ruled A.D. 98–117) and Hadrian (ruled A.D. 117–138).

Philosophers and Gladiators

Spain also gave the Roman world a large number of outstanding intellectual and cultural figures. The most famous of these were Quintilian (A.D. 35–c. 195), the leading Roman writer on rhetoric and education; the philosopher Seneca the Elder (c. 4 B.C.–A.D. 65); and his son Seneca the Younger, the tutor of the emperor Nero. Others were the poets Lucan and Martial, the agronomist Columella, and the geographer Pomponius Mela.

This high culture was the realm of a tiny elite. For the vast majority of the people in towns Roman culture meant free public entertainments, such as animal baiting, chariot races, and gladiatorial combats. (The little we know about the actual gladiators comes from a few surviving epitaphs. For example, Faustus, a slave from Egypt, died in the ring in Córdoba after twelve fights.) These were sponsored by private individuals or by the towns. Magistrates had to sponsor at least one set of games, which could last for four days, each year. They were held in the arenas and amphitheaters, which could hold up to thirty thousand people and were part of all Romanized towns.

The most visible remaining evidence of Roman cultural influence is architectural: theaters, amphitheaters, arenas, bridges, aqueducts, and private homes. Roman styles were introduced by Italian settlers and then copied by wealthy Spaniards who sought to glorify themselves and their hometowns.

The elite were urban, but from the second century A.D. on they fled from the towns and the bothers of local office to their country estates, or villas. There they had luxurious mansions built to reproduce the comforts of town life.

The End of Roman Spain

The collapse of Roman power began in 409 and ended in 475. In A.D. 406 the Vandals, Suebi, and Alans, whom the Romans called barbarians, crossed the Rhine River

The Roman aqueduct at Segovia. This photograph was taken in the 1890's. Biblioteca Nacional, Madrid

Romans used mosaics, such as this one, to decorate the floors of houses and public buildings. Museo Arqueológico Nacional, Madrid

into the empire. Three years later they entered Spain, and by 411 only one of the five provinces, Tarraconensis, remained under Roman control. The Romans were unable to defeat the invaders themselves, so they called on another people, the Visigoths, to do it for them. In 456 the Visigoths pushed the Suebi into Gallaecia and within ten years had taken control of all the rest of Spain, except Tarraconensis, the last Roman stronghold. That fell to the Visigoths in 475. The entire western Roman empire disappeared the following year.

Visigothic Spain

The Visigoths were outnumbered by the Romanized Spaniards by at least ten to one. Until the middle of the seventh century they maintained two distinct legal and administrative systems. According to a modern historian, "the Gothic nobility governed the Gothic population and the Roman nobility the Roman population, while the Gothic king and his highest officials decided policy for them all."

The Visigoths were culturally distinct from the Romanized Spaniards and proud of it. Even when they moved into the towns next to Hispano-Roman elite they maintained their language, their clothing, and their laws. They even chose a different brand of Christianity. This was Arianism, which was a heresy in the eyes of the Roman church.

Over time, however, they became more and more Romanized. By the end of the sixth century Gothic styles of clothing and art had largely disappeared and been replaced by ones from the eastern Roman empire. One scholar has said that this Roman influence was so strong that if one had only the archaeological evidence, one would not guess that Germans had ruled Spain after 600.

Unified Spain   The political unity of Spain was restored by the Visigothic king Leovigild (ruled 568–586) who defeated the Suebic

Isidore of Seville

The leading intellectual figure of Visigothic Spain was Isidore of
Seville. He is believed to have been born around 560. Nothing certain
is known about his life before he became Bishop of Seville in 599 or
600, succeeding his brother Leander, although it is believed that he
had been a monk.

Isidore's written works are voluminous and varied. His most famous
book was the *Etymologies*, a twenty-volume compilation of all branches
of knowledge based on the etymologies of words. It remained influential
throughout the Middle Ages. He also wrote historical chronicles, such
as the *History of the Goths, Vandals and Suevi*, and a large number of
ecclesiastical works. Among these are *On the Offices of the Church*,
which describes the various categories of clergy and church services,
and *On the Christian Faith, Against the Jews*, which uses the Old
Testament in an effort to refute Jewish arguments against Christianity.

Isidore was also an influential political figure. He emerged as ad-
viser to the king on religious and scholarly matters during the reign of
Sisebut (612–621), and he retained his influence at court until his
death in 636.

kingdom of Galicia in 585. His son, Reccared (ruled 586–601), imposed a new kind of unity on the kingdom, the unity of a single religion. The Visigoths were Arians, Christians who did not believe,
as Catholics did, that the Son and the Holy Ghost were the equals
of the Father. Leovigild had sought to reinforce Arianism against
Catholicism, but the conversion of his son, King Reccared, in 587
meant that Arianism was doomed. This was confirmed at the Third

"The World"
From *Etymologies:*

> The world is what endures in the heavens and on earth, in the sea and the stars. It is called the world, *mundus*, because it is always in motion, *motus*; no rest is ever allowed it.

"King Reccared converts to Christianity"
From *History of the Goths, Vandals and Suevi:*

> After the death of Leovigild, his son Reccared was crowned with kingship; he was endowed with reverence for religion and was greatly different from his father in character. For the latter was irreligious and very much disposed to war, while he was devout in faith and renowned for his love of peace; his father by the skills of war expanded the rule of his nation, while he with greater glory elevated the same nation by the victory of faith. For at the very beginning of his reign he embraced the Catholic faith and after removing the sin of their deep-rooted error he brought back the people of the whole Gothic nation to reverence for the true faith.

Council of Toledo in 589, although some Arian bishops and noblemen did rebel. Finally, in 654 Recceswinth (ruled 653–672) ended the dual legal and administrative system by abolishing Roman law and with it the positions that had been held by the Roman nobility.

The Visigoths had succeeded in imposing both political and religious unity on Spain, although the Basques remained pagans and free from central authority. Such unity could be maintained only through the use of coercion against those who dissented. The principal targets were the Jews, who had been in Spain since at least the first century A.D. From the very moment the monarchy became Catholic, it began to persecute the Jews with laws that became more sweeping and violent as time went on, including one that decreed the death sentence for celebrating either the Jewish Sabbath or Passover.

The Visigoths achieved a lot, but their rule did not last long. In 711, only 110 years after the death of Reccared, both the Visigothic kingdom and Spanish unity were shattered by new invaders bringing a new culture and a new religion.

In large part, the rapidity of the Visigoths' defeat was due to the tensions in their increasingly repressive society. The Jews must have welcomed the invaders, since their position could only improve. The large slave population was also a problem. Law after law in the sixth and seventh centuries dealt with the question of runaway slaves and imposed ever harsher and more sweeping penalties for not turning them in. Visigothic Spain was already in crisis. Historian E. A. Thompson writes, "Slaves can no longer be bound to their work. They have already escaped in masses. [The king] himself admits that there is not a city, a fort, village or villa where they are not hiding. What will their attitude be when the Arabs land at Gibraltar?"

Conquest and Reconquest

The Emergence of Islam

The invaders were Moslems, followers of a religion called Islam. Like the Phoenicians, Greeks, Carthaginians, Romans, and Visigoths they came from the east. Unlike any of the others they were driven by a religious mission.

Islam was created by Mohammed (570–632), an Arab who believed he had received visions from the Archangel Gabriel. Mohammed saw himself as the last in a line of prophets that included Abraham, Moses, and Jesus, and he saw his message as a renewal of Judaism and Christianity. As believers in the "true" religion, Moslems felt they had the right to wage holy war against others. Moslems also distinguished two groups among the nonbelievers: Jews and Christians, whom they called the "people of the book," and everyone else. These two groups were to be treated differently when they came under Islamic rule. The "people of the book" would be allowed to practice their religions; the others had to choose between conversion and death.

Mohammed converted some of the Arab tribes, but his successors launched wars of conquest that rapidly took the new religion north, east, and west. By the end of the seventh century the Moslem empire, which was ruled from Damascus by the Ummayad dynasty, had spread across North Africa. Spain was the next obvious target.

The Conquest

There is more legend than hard knowledge about the Moslem conquest of Spain. The most common story is that Count Julian, the governor of the city of Ceuta in Morocco, helped the Moslems in order to avenge himself on the Spanish King, Rodrigo, who had seduced his daughter.

Rodrigo had been crowned King of Spain in 710. He began his reign, as had so many of his predecessors, campaigning against the Basques in the north, but in 711 he received word of a new enemy. Tariq, in command of a force of between 1,700 and 7,000 men, had crossed over from North Africa, landed at Gibraltar ("Rock of Tariq" in Arabic), and begun to march north. Rodrigo rushed south to confront the invader. Toward the end of April 711 the two forces fought near the Guadalete River. Rodrigo's army was defeated, and he died in the battle.

With its ruler defeated and killed, the Visigothic kingdom could put up very little resistance, especially since many Visigothic nobles made deals with the invaders. Tariq continued on to Toledo, which he found undefended. His master, Musa ibn Nusayr, the Arab governor of North Africa, brought over a larger army to continue the conquest. By 715 they had subdued almost the entire peninsula. They then crossed the

Pyrenees into France, but by 759 they had been thrown out. Arabs would remain in Spain for more than seven hundred years.

Initially Spain—Al-Andalus was its Arabic name—was ruled by the caliph in Damascus through a governor who had his capital in Córdoba. In the 740's, however, Al-Andalus was rocked by a series of civil wars caused by racial differences among the conquerors. All were Moslems, but they were divided between a minority who were Arabs and the majority who were Berber tribesmen from North Africa. Though the Berbers had resisted the Arabs longer than any other people, the Arabs looked down on them as racially inferior. In 739 the Berbers in North Africa rebelled, and the revolt quickly spread to Spain. The struggle continued for nearly twenty years.

The fate of Al-Andalus was affected by events in faraway Damascus. The last Ummayad caliph of Damascus was overthrown in 750, and all the members of his family but one were murdered. The one who escaped, Abd al-Rahman, took refuge with the Berbers in North Africa. One contemporary chronicle recounted his escape, including the following episode, supposedly told in Abd al-Rahman's own words:

We reached the bank of the Euphrates [river]. . . . Next we heard the noise of the troop approaching. . . . We took to our heels and hid in some gardens by the Euphrates, but they were closing in on us. We managed to reach the river ahead of them and threw ourselves into the water. When they got to the bank they began shouting: "Come back; you have nothing to fear." Half way across I turned to encourage [my brother]; but on hearing their promises he had turned back, afraid of drowning. I shouted to him but God did not will that he heard me. I swam on to the opposite bank. Then I saw that the soldiers were undressing to swim after me. They stopped, caught the boy and cut off his head in front of me. He was thirteen years old.

From North Africa he crossed into Spain in 756, defeated the Caliph's governor, and declared himself Emir, ruling as Abd al-Rahman I until 788. In 929 Abd al-Rahman III declared himself Caliph, a title which included religious as well as military and political authority.

Ummayad Spain

The Ummayad dynasty that Abd al-Rahman founded ruled Al-Andalus until 1031, and under their rule it was one of the wealthiest and most powerful states in Europe. Still, it was not free from internal problems. There were conflicts between the Berbers and the local Spaniards and others among different Arab groups. There were also revolts by local governors who resisted control from the capital. Al-Hakam I, who had to confront these disturbances, later tried to explain his ruthlessness in a letter to his son and successor:

As the tailor uses his needle to sew together pieces of cloth, so did I employ my sword in order to unite the divided provinces. . . . Ask now, what are my frontiers, whether there is any one place that lies in the power of the enemy— they will answer you no. Yet if they were to answer you with yes, I would fly there immediately, clad in my suit of armor, sword in hand. Ask, also, of the skulls of the rebellious subjects, that lie scattered on the plain, like gourds split in two, shining in the sunlight. They will tell you that it was I who slew them without hesitation. . . . If I spared neither their women nor their children, it was because they threatened my own family; he who does not avenge injustice done to his own family has no feeling of honor, and is despised by everyman.

The Reconquest

Finally there was the question of the relations between Al-Andalus and the Christian states. The Moslem conquest had pushed the Christians into isolated mountain strongholds in the far north of the peninsula. Some were descendants of those who had most strongly resisted the Romans and the Visigoths; others were refugees from the south. These people led what is called the *Reconquista*, the reconquest of the peninsula by Christian princes, which was completed only in 1492.

The Reconquest was not carried out by a single Christian state but by a number of them. The first was the kingdom of Asturias, which became the kingdom of León and then the kingdom of Castile. The counties of Aragon and Catalonia were first established by the Franks during the reign of Charlemagne at the end of the eighth century and evolved into the kingdom of Aragon. The small kingdom of Navarre emerged in the tenth century. Portugal separated from Castile and became an independent state in the twelfth century. Though they all fought against the Moslems, the Christian rulers were rivals, frequently fighting each other as they sought to extend their own realms.

The Reconquest began in 722, when a Gothic noble named Pelayo (718–737) defeated a Moslem force at Covadonga, in the mountains of Asturias. For the Moslems this was a small and unimportant setback; for the Christians it made possible the creation of the kingdom of Asturias under Alfonso I (739–757) and symbolized their struggle against Islam.

The relations between Al-Andalus and the Christians were not inevitably hostile. Religion was not an absolute line of division. The Christians recognized the superior power of Al-Andalus and frequently asked its rulers to intervene in their internal struggles, especially when these involved disputes over who should succeed to the throne.

Sancho "the Fat"

When Ramiro II of León died in 955, Sancho I ("the Fat") and Ordoño IV ("the Bad") both claimed the throne. After ruling for two years Sancho, who was so fat that he could not ride a horse and could barely walk, was overthrown and replaced by Ordoño. His uncle, the King of Navarre, suggested that Sancho seek the help of the Caliph of Córdoba. The Caliph's doctor, who was Jewish, helped Sancho lose weight, and in 960 he was returned to the throne with the help of a Moslem army. Ordoño, who was now out of a job,

The monument to Pelayo at Covadonga, where the Reconquest began. Agueda Shubert

The Power of Al-Andalus

The Arab historian Ibn Hayyan recounts the story of the visit of Ordoño IV to the Caliph Al-Hakem II in 961. Ordoño's behavior illustrates the grandeur of the Caliph's court and the much greater power of his state.

[Ordoño said] I am the slave of the Commander of the Faithful, my lord and master, and I come to implore his favor, to witness his majesty and to place myself and my people under his protection. May he be pleased to grant me his powerful patronage and consent to receive me into the number of his slaves. [Ordoño] rose to retire, walking backwards so as not to turn his face from the caliph. . . . He plainly exhibited on his countenance. . . his utter astonishment at the magnificence and splendor displayed before him as indicative of the power and strength of the Caliphate. In passing through the hall, his eyes fell on the vacant throne of the [caliph]; unable to repress his feelings he advanced slowly towards it, and having prostrated himself before it remained for some time as if the caliph were sitting on it.

turned to Córdoba for help, but he died before anything could be done.

The glory of the caliphate and the power of Al-Andalus both came to an end not long after this. For the next twenty years one caliph followed another on an almost annual basis before the caliphate disintegrated entirely in 1031.

Taifa Kingdoms

From 1031 until 1085 Islamic Spain was made up of a large number of small kingdoms, known as *taifas*. There were more than twenty *taifas* at first, but as a result of the wars they continually fought among themselves the weakest ones were taken over by the strongest, who frequently hired Christian warriors to help them. By 1085 there were only eleven left.

The collapse of the caliphate of Córdoba and the chaos that followed allowed the Christian states to take the initiative. Castile and Aragon were able to push to the south, and in 1085 the Castilians took the old Visigothic capital of Toledo. The petty kings were desperate. In 1085 they requested help from the Almoravids, Berber nomads and puritanical Moslems who had conquered most of North Africa. The decision was not an easy one for the *taifa* kings. They disliked the Almoravids, whom they considered barbarians, almost as much as they disliked the idea of coming under the authority of a Christian ruler. The Almoravids defeated Alfonso VI of Castile in 1086, temporarily halting the Christian advance. Over the next fifteen years the Almoravids deposed the *taifa* kings and brought all Al-Andalus under one ruler once again.

El Cid

It was against the Almoravids that the greatest Christian warrior of the Reconquest, and one of Spain's greatest heroes, won his victories. This was Rodrigo Díaz de Vivar, known as El Cid, from *Sidi*, "My Lord" in Arabic. El Cid's career reveals the complexities of the Spanish Reconquest. Christians were not always fighting Moslems: At times they fought among themselves and cooperated with the Moslems.

On his death in 1065 Ferdinand I divided his kingdom between his two sons; Castile went to Sancho II and León to Alfonso VI. The brothers immediately fought, and El Cid, fighting for Sancho, twice defeated Alfonso in battle. Alfonso eventually won, and he exiled El Cid twice. During his first exile he served the Emir of Zaragoza, fighting against both the Moslem Emir of Elerida and the Christian Count of Barcelona. During his second exile he fought the Count of Barcelona once again,

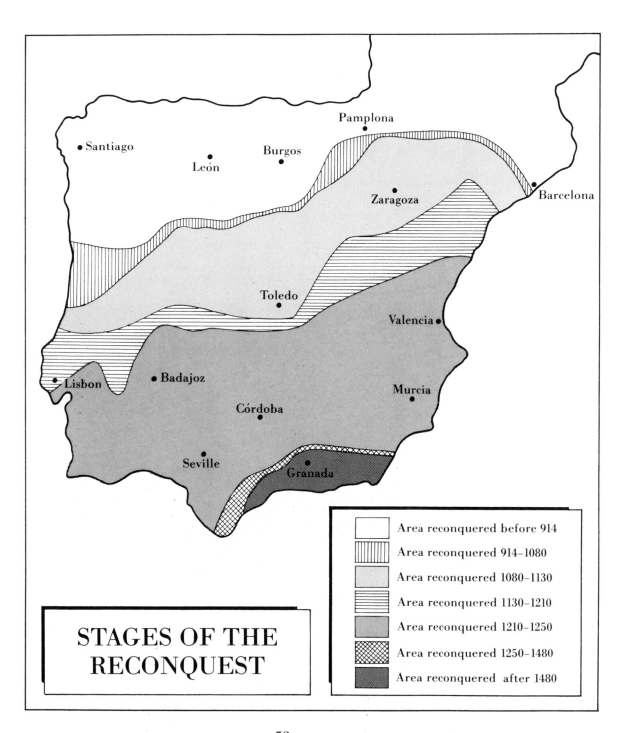

STAGES OF THE
RECONQUEST

Area reconquered before 914

Area reconquered 914–1080

Area reconquered 1080–1130

Area reconquered 1130–1210

Area reconquered 1210–1250

Area reconquered 1250–1480

Area reconquered after 1480

Santiago

León

Burgos

Pamplona

Zaragoza

Barcelona

Toledo

Valencia

Lisbon

Badajoz

Córdoba

Murcia

Seville

Granada

but in 1094 he captured Valencia from the Moslems after a two-year siege. He ruled the city until his death in 1099. His widow, Jimena, ruled for three more years until the city was taken by the Almoravids.

The story of El Cid is best known from the epic poem *Cantar del Mio Cid (Poem of the Cid)*. The poem was written about a hundred years after the warrior's death and it presented a picture of the Cid that differed in important ways from the life of the historical figure. The real Cid was cruel and opportunistic, a knight on the make who fought for whoever paid him and wherever it was to his advantage. Once he even attacked the kingdom of his nominal lord, Alfonso VI of Castile. In contrast, the Cid of the poem is a true Castilian, a crusading Christian, and a loyal subject.

The fictional Cid was made into the Castilian national hero, the embodiment of the true Castilian—and, by extension, Spanish—character. This version was most compellingly presented by the historian Ramón Menéndez Pidal (1869–1968) in his study *The Spain of the Cid*, which was published in 1929. Undoubtedly the most widely known representation of El Cid is the movie of the same name, in which Charlton Heston played the title role. Menéndez Pidal was the historical consultant for the film, and Heston's Cid is very much his perfect Castilian hero.

At War

The Almoravids had stopped the Christian advance, but only briefly. Zaragoza fell to Alfonso I of Aragon in 1118, pushing Moslem rule south of the Ebro River. The population of Al-Andalus also became dissatisfied with the Almoravids, and a series of revolts in 1144 and 1145 broke their state apart and led to the creation of a new set of *taifa* kingdoms.

Jihad   The situation became more complicated in 1147. During the previous twenty-five years a new Moslem sect, the Almohads, had defeated the Almoravid empire in North Africa. They then invaded Al-Andalus and quickly defeated the Almoravids in Seville. They also defeated a number of the new petty kingdoms.

Almohad Islam was what is known as a *jihad* movement—that is, a

---

Poem of the Cid

El Cid defeats the Almoravids at Valencia:

> The Cid had roused [King Yusuf's] anger and he said: "He has forcibly invaded my territory and he attributes all his success to Jesus Christ." So the Moorish king assembled his armed forces, 50,000 strong, and they embarked in ships and set sail for Valencia in search of the Cid. When the ships arrived they disembarked.
>
> All the men, fully armed, went out by the towers of Valencia, the Cid meanwhile giving them advice and instructions. . . . The Cid sallied forth, mounted on Babieca and wearing his full armor. They left Valencia with their standard carried in front, four thousand in all but thirty forming the Cid's company, going eagerly to the attack of 50,000 Moors. . . . The Cid first used his lance and then wielded his sword, killing countless Moors while the blood dripped down to his elbow. He struck three blows at King Yusuf but the king escaped the Cid's sword and galloped off on his swift horse, not stopping until he was inside the fine fortress of Cullera.

movement whose goal was to re-create a purified Islamic society. Almohads believed in the strict application of the *sharia*, the Islamic law that governed all aspects of social life. This included giving men and women separate social roles, the imposition of modest forms of dress for women, and prohibitions on alcohol and dancing. The Almohads were so intolerant of the laxity of the Spanish Moslems that they declared that all non-Almohads were infidels and could have their property confiscated.

In practice, Islamic law was not applied equally to everyone. The masses were subject to it but an enlightened minority was allowed greater freedom, especially in the realm of intellectual activity. The contradiction was apparent in the career of Averroës, the greatest philosopher of Islamic Spain. When he was not engaging in wide-ranging philosophic speculations, he was carrying out his obligations as a government official responsible for applying the *sharia*.

Christian Conquests

While all this was going on, the Christians were able to make important new conquests. Afonso Henriques, who had been recognized as King of Portugal in 1143, took Lisbon in 1147. Later that year Almería fell to Alfonso VII of Castile and Ramón Berenguer IV of Catalonia, and by 1149 Berenguer had won a series of victories to throw the Moslems out of the Ebro valley.

Once the Almohads had established their control over Al-Andalus, they turned on the Christians. Their raids into Christian-held territory were answered by Christians' raids into theirs, including an attack on Seville. The Almohads' greatest victory, and what would be the last major Moslem victory in Spain, came in 1195 at Alarcos, near Ciudad Real. The Caliph, Al-Mansur, routed Alfonso VIII of Castile but then returned to Seville. Had he taken advantage of the disorganization of his enemy by pushing on to the Castilian capital of Toledo, Spanish history might have been different.

After a period of peace in 1209 the Christian kings responded to the Pope's call for a new crusade and attacked once again. Aragon and Navarre assisted Castile, as did volunteers from across Europe. The Christian and Moslem armies met on July 13, 1212, at Las Navas de Tolosa.

The battle was a victory for the Christians, by far the greatest and most important of the Reconquest. The power of the Almohads was broken, a new set of *taifa* kingdoms emerged, and within fifty years the Christian kingdoms had taken almost all of Al-Andalus. James I ("the Conqueror") of Aragon won the Balearic Islands in 1229 and Valencia in 1238. Under Ferdinand III Castile conquered the two former Moslem capitals, Córdoba in 1236 and Seville in 1248. His son, the future Alfonso X ("the Wise"), captured Murcia in 1244. Only the kingdom of Granada remained under Moslem rule; it would survive until 1492.

The Reconquest brought vast amounts of land into Christian hands. What did they do with it?

Knights and Lords in Christian Spain

The kings of Castile claimed the right to distribute conquered land. In northern Castile the nobility received a healthy share, but so too did numerous individuals who dared settle on the frontier. They valued their property and their liberty and resisted attempts by noblemen to control them.

Things were different in the south. There the amount of land available was far greater than the number of people to occupy it. In addition, the south remained a military frontier for almost three centuries. Castilian kings distributed the land in immense blocs to individual nobles, to the Church, and to three military orders. The orders of Alcántara, Calátrava, and Santiago had been created in the twelfth century as organizations of knights committed to fighting the Moslems and defending the frontier. These grants of land to nobility, Church, and knightly orders were the origins of great estates that would endure over many centuries and come to cause major social and political problems.

By this time the political structure of the peninsula had been set. Castile was the largest of the kingdoms and the only one that had a border with the Moslem state of Granada. Aragon and Catalonia had been united by marriage in 1137, but the union was purely a dynastic one; the two realms retained different laws, political institutions, and languages. Portugal had been recognized as a separate kingdom in 1143 and Navarre remained a small, independent state.

Birth of an Empire

For the kings of Aragon the Reconquest was over. They now turned their attention outward, to the Mediterranean basin. In the past Spain had been conquered by more powerful states to the east. Now, for the first time a Spanish kingdom set out to build an empire outside the peninsula.

In 1282 Pedro III ("the Great") conquered Sicily, which earned him excommunication by Pope Martin IV. By the end of the century members of the Aragonese dynasty also controlled Sardinia and Corsica. In the first years of the fourteenth century the Catalan Company, a group of free-lance soldiers, took control of the Duchy of Athens and held it for seventy years in the name of the Aragonese King of Sicily.

Both Castile and Aragon endured repeated political instability and even civil war from the late thirteenth to the mid-fifteenth century. The two kingdoms suffered from popular uprisings, revolts by the nobility against royal power and, most frequently, disputes over the succession to the throne.

In 1369 Enrique Trastámara took the throne of Castile after killing

The Political Development of Christian Spain

737	Kingdom of Asturias created by Alfonso I
801	County of Barcelona created by Bera
810	Kingdom of Navarre created by Iñigo Iñiguez Arista
878	Title of Count of Barcelona made hereditary by Wilfred "the Hairy"
910	Kingdom of León created by García
1035	Kingdom of Aragon created by Ramiro I
1035	Kingdom of Castile created by Ferdinand I
1037	Unification of Castile and León by Ferdinand I
1137	Unification of Aragon and Catalonia
1143	Kingdom of Portugal created by Afonso Henriques
1158	Separation of León and Castile
1230	Reunification of León and Castile by Ferdinand III
1469	Marriage of Isabella of Castile and Ferdinand of Aragon

his half-brother, Pedro "the Cruel," with his own hands. Fernando of Antequera, the brother of Enrique III of Castile, was chosen King of Aragon in 1412. The Trastámara dynasty used marriages to restore the unity of Spain. Portugal remained apart.

Unity was realized in 1469 when Isabella of Castile married her cousin, Ferdinand of Aragon. During the 1460's there was civil war in both Castile and Aragon. Not everyone accepted Ferdinand and Isabella as the heirs to their respective kingdoms, but they both overcame the challenges to their rights. Isabella came to the throne in

Isabella of Castile

As Queen of Castile from 1474 until 1504, Isabella oversaw the union of the crowns of Castile and Aragon, the completion of the Reconquest, and the arrival of the Europeans in America. She is generally considered to have been one of the greatest—if not the greatest—of Spain's rulers.

Isabella is best known for her fierce piety and devotion to Catholicism as well as for her personal virtue. Even so, she was not as dour a person as her faith, and her portraits, would lead us to believe. Her husband, Ferdinand, was quite the ladies' man; she put up with his frequent affairs, but took her revenge where she could. According to one Italian contemporary, "her jealousy was so strong that if she suspected that [Ferdinand] was getting too interested in one of the ladies at court, she would find a discreet way of having the woman dismissed from court." She had one of these women, Beatriz de Bobadilla, shipped off to the Canary Islands.

The daily life of the royal household was relatively modest, but special state occasions were exceptionally lavish and Isabella took full advantage of the opportunity to dress appropriately. A contemporary chronicle records that for a jousting tournament that lasted two days "the Queen was dressed in brocade and wore a crown. . . . She rode a horse which had a coverlet and whose mane, bridle and halter were decorated with silver and golden flowerlets." Following a reception for the representatives of Charles VIII of France, her confessor criticized her for overdoing it. She responded in a letter: "You have been told things which did not happen. . . . Neither I nor my ladies wore new dresses. All the clothes I wore I had had since arriving in Aragon and the Frenchmen had already seen me in the outfit I wore that night, which was made of silk and as plain as could be. . . . As to the men's clothes, which were extremely expensive, I did not order them; in fact I did everything I could to prevent them being made."

1474, although her husband had to defeat an invasion by Afonso V of Portugal in 1475. Ferdinand became King of Aragon in 1479.

Of the entire peninsula, only the tiny kingdom of Granada remained under Moslem rule. Faced with the overwhelming military power of the Christian kingdoms and the determination of their rulers to make all of Spain Catholic, its defeat was only a matter of time.

Moslem Spain/ Christian Spain

Moslem Spain

Until the decisive Christian onslaught at the beginning of the thirteenth century, Al-Andalus enjoyed a brilliant culture, superior to that of Christian Spain. Under the Ummayad caliphs, many of whom were scholars and great patrons of the arts, Córdoba became a great center of Moslem learning. Whether it was ruled by a single government or a series of petty kingdoms, Spain remained a cultural capital of the Islamic world.

Moslem writers created new forms of poetry in both classical and colloquial Arabic. One of the great themes of the poetry of Al-Andalus was courtly love, which idealized women and spoke of spiritual rather than physical love. This also became a major theme in medieval European lyric poetry. Some have argued that the Christians got the idea from Islamic Spain. This is open to debate, but there is no question that the Arabic language had a major influence on the development of Spanish. All Spanish words which begin with "al" come from Arabic, where "al" means "the." Almost four thousand Spanish words, dealing with things such as the sciences, government, the home, agriculture, architecture, and the military, come from Arabic; only Latin gave Spanish more words. Many of these words, such as cotton *(algodón)*, rice *(arroz)*, and orange *(naranja)*, then passed into English and other European languages.

Arts and Sciences

Beginning with a scientist named Maslama (d. 1007), Spanish Moslems developed important schools of astronomy and mathematics and produced very high quality astrolabes and quadrants, the instruments

Some Words of Arabic Origin in Spanish

alcalde	mayor	*aduana*	customs
alcohol	alcohol	*alambique*	still
algebra	algebra	*alhaja*	jewel
jarra	jug	*taza*	cup
alfombra	carpet	*alfareria*	pottery
almohada	pillow	*ajedrez*	chess
aceituna	olive	*arroz*	rice
azucar	sugar	*zanahoria*	carrot
laud	lute	*tambor*	drum
alferez	lieutenant	*atalaya*	watchtower

sailors employed to determine their position using the stars.

The most important contribution of Al-Andalus to Christian culture in Spain, and beyond, was the recovery of the works of classical Greek philosophy, especially those of Aristotle. A number of Moslem thinkers tried to make Aristotle's ideas fit with those of their religion. The most famous of these scholars were Avicenna (d. 1037) and Ibn Rushd, known as Averroës (1126–1198), but their efforts to reconcile reason with religion were not always well received by other Moslems.

The Commentator

Averroës had a major influence on Christian thought through his commentaries on the work of Aristotle. Both Dante, the author of *The Divine Comedy*, and Saint Thomas Aquinas, perhaps the greatest of all Catholic theologians, called him the "Commentator"; and in the thirteenth century many Christian writers did not really distinguish the writings of Averroës from those of Aristotle himself. Aquinas, among others, spent a lot of time trying to refute Averroës' ideas, which were seen as a threat to Christian beliefs because they put too much emphasis on human reason over faith.

The Moslems also left Spain a great cultural heritage in their architectural achievements. Some of the distinctive features of their architecture were the use of the horseshoe-shaped arch, the use of decorative tiles, and enclosed courtyards with fountains. Their mosques and palaces are among the most famous and beautiful buildings in Spain. Notable examples include the great mosque of Córdoba and the palace of the kings of Granada, the Alhambra.

Spanish Christians did not value this heritage. Some buildings, such as the Alhambra, were ignored and allowed to decay until western interest in the Moorish past revived in the nineteenth century. (One of the first people to "rediscover" the Alhambra was the American writer Washington Irving.) Other buildings, such as mosques, were converted into churches. In the case of the Córdoba mosque, this meant adding walls to a building that had had none. The conversion destroyed the original design, in which the rows of columns in the mosque were continued in the rows of orange trees in the surrounding courtyard.

The Islamic invaders were always a minority among the population of Al-Andalus, and they themselves were ethnically divided, including Arabs, Berbers, Syrians, and others. Many Christian Spaniards left for Christian-controlled territory, but the majority converted to Islam and were eventually assimilated into Moslem society

Mozárabes and Jews

Even those who did not convert were increasingly influenced by the Arabic language and culture. These remaining Christians within Al-Andalus were known as *mozárabes*. In the tenth century many fled to Christian Spain, taking with them distinctive forms of architecture and art.

Under the Ummayads the two religious minorities, Christians and Jews, were quite well treated. Like all nonbelievers in Islamic countries, they were subject to a special tax, but with few exceptions they were not persecuted or pressured to convert. Members of both religions could attain important positions at court.

Maimonides   The tenth, eleventh and twelfth centuries were a high point for Jews in Moslem Spain and one of the great periods of Jewish cultural achievement anywhere. The most outstanding figure was Moses Maimonides (d. 1204). Like his Moslem contemporary, Averroës, Maimonides was from Córdoba and a doctor. Both men tried to eliminate the contradictions between the faith demanded by their religions and the demands of reason laid out by Aristotle. This was not easy and could lead to confusion. The purpose of Maimonides's *Guide of the Perplexed* was to help overcome that conflict:

The Alhambra palace in Granada was one of the greatest architectural achievements of Islamic Spain. This photograph of the Patio of the Lions was taken in the 1890's. Biblioteca Nacional, Madrid

To give indications to a religious man for whom the validity of our [Jewish] Law has become established in his soul and has become actual in his belief . . . and having studied the sciences of the philosophers and come to know what they signify. The human intellect having drawn him on and led him to dwell within its province, he must have felt distressed by the externals of the Law. . . . Hence he would remain in a state of perplexity and confusion as to whether he should follow his intellect, renounce what he knew concerning the terms in question and consequently consider that he has renounced the foundations of the Law. Or should he hold fast to his understanding of these terms and not let himself be drawn on together with his intellect, rather turning his back on it and moving away from it, while at the same time perceiving that he had brought loss to himself and harm to his religion?

The great mosque of Córdoba in a photograph taken in the 1890's. The horseshoe arch was one of the characteristic features of Moorish architecture. Biblioteca Nacional, Madrid

Both Maimonides and Averroës were attacked by members of their own faiths who found their approach too rationalistic. Both ended their lives in exile, forced to flee from Córdoba because of persecution by religious fanatics.

Christian Spain

Over the course of the Reconquest Christian Spain developed from a poor and backward society to a complex and sophisticated one with a distinguished culture. In the twelfth and thirteenth centuries Toledo was the center where Christian scholars met Jews and Moslems and where the superior knowledge of the Islamic world was acquired by the Christian world. Much of the culture of ancient Greece—such as the philosophy of Aristotle, which had been lost since the barbarian invasions—was recovered by the west through Arabic translations, which were then translated into Latin.

The Moslem world was not the only cultural influence on Christian Spain. Christian Europe also contributed a lot. The most striking influence was the introduction of the Romanesque and Gothic styles of church architecture. These came mostly from France, brought by the thousands of pilgrims who, from the eleventh century on, flocked to the shrine of Santiago de Compostela, where the body of Saint James is supposedly buried. The Romanesque and Gothic cathedrals still stand all along the "French Road," which passed through Burgos, León, Logroño, and Oviedo before reaching Santiago.

Latin remained the language of the world of scholarship, literature, government, and the Church through the twelfth century. One significant exception was the *Poem of the Cid*, probably composed in the first half of the twelfth century.

Between the thirteenth and fifteenth centuries Castilians and

Catalonians created a varied and distinguished literature in their own languages. (These languages of daily life and not of high learning are known as vernacular languages.) In both cases the royal courts stimulated the use of these vernacular languages. In Castile the most important rulers were Ferdinand III (ruled 1217–1252) and Alfonso X ("the Wise") (ruled 1252–1284); in Aragon it was James I ("the Conqueror") (ruled 1213–1276).

Book of Good Love

The earliest Spanish literature dealt with religious themes and moral philosophy. Lyric and courtly poetry continued to be written in Gallego, the language of Galicia, until the middle of the fourteenth century. Then stories of chivalry, inspired by the Crusades and largely based on French models, began to appear.

The greatest literary work of the fourteenth century, *Book of Good Love*, by Juan Ruiz, the Archpriest of Hita, fits no simple category. His book is a collection of poems about love that puts bawdy stories, such as one in which the Archpriest "takes part in the blasphemous triumphal entry of the god of love," alongside songs to the Virgin Mary which include lines such as

> *Holy Virgin, chosen*
> *by God his beloved Mother*
> *exalted in heaven*
> *life and health from the world.*

Because of this unusual mixture of elements it has been seen as a parody, a guide to love, or a moral tale.

In the fifteenth century the ballad became the most popular form of

The Gothic style, with its simple but graceful arches, was introduced into Spain from France. Here is the interior of the cathedral of Barcelona. Courtesy of the Tourist Office of Spain

Pilgrims from across Christian Europe were drawn to the shrine of Santiago de Compostela. It remains an important pilgrimage destination for Catholics today.
Courtesy of the Tourist Office of Spain

poetry, at least among ordinary people. These ballads were usually short and dealt with a wide variety of themes, such as historical or legendary subjects and events on the military frontier.

The political upheavals of the fourteenth and fifteenth centuries inspired a large number of chronicles. The best known author of such chronicles was Pedro López de Ayala (1332–1407), whose *Rhyme of the Palace* described life at the court of the Trastámara kings. Politics also inspired much of the work of the elite poets of the period, men like the Marqués de Santillana (1398–1458) and Juan de Mena (1411–1456).

The unification of the crowns coincided with the publication of Antonio de Nebrija's *Grammar of the Castilian Language*. This was the first significant work of Spanish grammar and the first attempt to define standard spelling and sentence structure.

Sighs from Afar   The first examples of Catalan literature were the poems of the troubadors. This lyric poetry dealt with themes of ideal love and moral questions and was written in a language heavily influenced by the Provençal spoken in southern France. The following lines come from the early-fifteenth-century poet Jordi de Sant Jordi:

> *I often sigh for you from afar, my lady,*
> *And sighing, my madness grows,*
> *For your love which punishes me so strongly*
> *That I go round in great melancholy.*

Catalan

Prose was being written in Catalan by the thirteenth century. One of the most highly developed forms of writing was the chronicle. Four great medieval Catalan chronicles survive: James I's *Book of Deeds*, and

A Philosopher King:
Alfonso X ("the Wise")

Alfonso X was a warrior who vigorously carried on the Reconquest and a ruler of vast ambition who for twenty years sought to have his claim to the title of Holy Roman Emperor accepted. We can get a clue to his personality from the fact that he personally knighted himself using a mechanical statue of Saint James and then crowned himself when he became King.

Alfonso was also a patron of scholarship and a man of learning, a writer and a translator in his own right. He founded a Latin-Arabic university in Seville and maintained a court of translators in Toledo. His own works included the Castilian law code *Las Siete Partidas*, works of history such as the *General Chronicle* and the *General History*, and translations of fiction and works on science and games from Arabic, among them the *Book of Chess*.

Alfonso's most famous work is the *Cántigas de Santa María*, written in 1279. This is a collection of 427 poems addressed to the Virgin Mary, written in Gallego and each set to its own music. The book includes illustrations of 1,300 scenes, many of them depicting the daily lives of people from all levels of society.

The Chronicle of Bernat Desclot, The Chronicle of Ramón Muntaner, and *The Chronicle of Peter III.* All record the achievements of the Aragonese and Catalans, both in their own countries and beyond, and glorify their kings. Two were written largely by the rulers themselves.

The last outstanding Catalan work of this period is the long novel

Tirant lo Blanc, which was published in 1490 and quickly translated into Spanish and Italian; a century later Cervantes, the author of *Don Quixote*, praised it mightily. The hero, a young nobleman named Tirant lo Blanc, goes to England, where he becomes a knight. He then participates in wars across the Mediterranean before taking command of the armies of the emperor of Constantinople and defeating the Turks. For this he is allowed to marry the emperor's daughter and is proclaimed Caesar. In the end he gets sick and dies, which causes his wife and father-in-law to die of grief.

The greatest medieval Catalan scholar was Ramón Llull (1232?–1315?). Around the age of thirty, Llull, a nobleman from the island of Majorca who served at the royal court, saw visions of Jesus and had a spiritual crisis, which led him to devote the rest of his life to fighting non-Catholic ideas, especially among the Moslems. His mission took him to Rome, Genoa, Naples, Tunis, and Cyprus. In Tunis he debated religious questions with Islamic scholars and was arrested. Llull's written work was massive; there are 243 known titles. Most were intended to use logic to fight errors of belief and to spread what he considered to be the true faith.

The Rise of Religious Intolerance

The Almoravids and the Almohads who dominated Al-Andalus between 1085 and 1212 were more fanatical and much less tolerant of religious minorities than their predecessors. Faced with increasing persecution many *mozárabes* fled to the Christian kingdoms. Many Jews also sought protection there.

The response of Christian rulers to these Jewish refugees, and then to the *moriscos*, the Moslems who became their subjects as they conquered more and more of Al-Andalus, was initially one of tolerance.

Leading Figures of Medieval Spanish Literature

Gonzalo de Berceo (d. *c.* 1265)
  First known vernacular poet in Spanish
Juan Ruiz, Archpriest of Hita (d. *c.* 1351)
  Book of Good Love
Juan Manuel (1282–1348)
  Count Lucanor
Pedro López de Ayala (1332–1407)
  Rhyme of the Palace
Alfonso Martínez de Toledo (1397/8–1468)
  Corbacho
Antonio de Nebrija (1444–1522)
  Grammar of the Castilian Language

Neither group was treated as fully equal to the Christians, but they did have legally recognized rights. Christian rulers frequently appointed Jews to important official positions despite the fact that a number of popes had prohibited this.

Religious tolerance, especially for the Jews, began to weaken in the fourteenth century and disappeared in the fifteenth. In 1391 popular discontent turned into a major assault against Jewish communities. Many escaped, some to Granada; many others converted. A few years later the legal rights of both Jews and Moslems were restricted.

Religious tensions continued in the fifteenth century, and those Jews who had converted—the *conversos* or *marranos*, as they were called—

came under increasing suspicion. (The remaining Moslems, or *mudéjares,* had much lower social status than either the Jews or the *conversos* and were rarely the targets of violence.) The unification of the kingdoms of Castile and Aragon under Ferdinand and Isabella was the death sentence for a multicultural Spain. Political unity demanded religious unity.

Leading Figures of Medieval Catalan Literature

James I ("the Conqueror") (1208–1276)
  Book of Deeds
Bernat Desclot
  The Chronicle of Bernat Desclot
Ramón Llull (1232?–1315?)
  Art of Finding the Truth; Book of Contemplation; Blanquerna; Book of the Lover and the Beloved
Ramón Muntaner (1265–1336)
  The Chronicle of Ramón Muntaner
Peter III (1239?–1285)
  The Chronicle of Peter III
Bernat Metge (d. 1413)
  The Dream
Ausías March (c.1395–c.1459)
  Songs of Love, Songs of Death, Song of the Spirit
Joan Martorell (c.1414–1468)
  Tirant lo Blanc

Inquisition

The tool for creating this unity was the Spanish Inquisition. Permission to set up such an institution was requested by Ferdinand and Isabella and granted by Pope Sixtus IV (1471–1484) in 1478. The court began to function in 1481. This new tribunal was not the only or even the first Inquisition; Pope Gregory IX (1227–1241) had created one in the thirteenth century to fight heresy.

The Spanish Inquisition was directed at the *conversos*, Jews who had converted to Catholicism but who were suspected of continuing to practice Judaism. (Later in its history it dealt with heretics of other sorts as well as moral and sexual deviants.)

The Inquisition accepted secret denunciations as evidence. It used torture and carried out its sentences, which included burning at the stake, in elaborate public ceremonies known as *autos-da-fé*, or acts of faith. The property of those who were found guilty was frequently confiscated.

These methods have made the Spanish Inquisition a synonym for cruelty and intolerance, but the Inquisition was very much an institution of its time, and perhaps even more humane than most. The torture was not supposed to kill or cause serious injury, and a doctor was available if something went wrong. There were very few cases of torture leading to death or even to broken limbs.

The Inquisition did not invent any especially diabolical tortures of its own, but used much the same ones as other religious and secular courts of the time. The most common were the *toca*, a form of water torture which consisted of having jars of water forced down one's throat; the *garrucha*, in which the victims were hung by the wrists, with weights attached to their feet, and then suddenly dropped; or the *potro*, in which the victim was stripped and bound to a rack by cords, which

From the Records of the Inquisition: The Trial of Juan González Daza, 1483–1484

Arraignment

I, Ferrand Rodrigues del Varco, Chaplain of our Lord the King and prosecutor of the Holy Inquisition . . . accuse Juan González Daza, resident of [Ciudad Real]. . . . Calling himself a Christian and enjoying the prerogatives of any Christian . . . he is guilty of judaizing and heresy for following the ceremonies of the Law of Moses, as follows:

1. He kept the Sabbath ceremony.

2. On Friday nights he allowed candles to be lit in his house.

3. He permitted food to be cooked in his house on Fridays to be eaten on Saturday in a ceremony.

4. He went to hear Jewish prayers on Friday nights with other *conversos.*

5. He ate meat during Lent and on days established by the Church for fasting.

A Witness for the Defense

Juan de Liébana said that . . . he has known Juan González Daza for 40 years and that he has always lived like a good Christian and gone to church like a faithful Christian . . . that he knows that he worked on Saturday as if it were like any other day . . . that he spent much time in his house and always saw that there were two candles lit at night. . . .

A Witness for the Prosecution

Antonia Martines . . . said under oath that when she was about 18 years old she lived in the house of Hernando de Theba and she saw that on the day of the Great Fast the wife of Juan Daza and his children came to beg pardon of the mother of de Theba and kiss her hand, because they were relatives and she put her hands on their heads. And she knows that Juan Daza, his wife and children kept the sabbath and she saw that on that day they did nothing but went to see relatives; and that on Friday they cooked food for Saturday and lit clean candles and kept the Jewish passover . . .

Confession

Juan González Daza was taken to the torture chamber and told to confess the truth of the charges of heresy against him. . . . He confessed nothing and was then put to the torment of the garrote. He then confessed. . . . He also said that when he went to church and prayed and heard mass he did not believe that the Messiah had come and that he went to Mass because he had the title of Christian.

Sentence

As the evidence of the witnesses presented by the prosecutor agrees with the confession of Juan González Daza, the accusation is well proven. . . . We decide that we must declare the said Juan González Daza to be and have been a heretic and apostate and we pronounce sentence of excommunication and all other spiritual and temporal penalties contained in the laws.

Juan González Daza was burned in the square of Ciudad Real on February 23, 1484.

were then tightened. Sentences which involved physical punishment were no more cruel than those meted out in other countries; there was nothing in the Inquisition's arsenal to equal the use of boiling lead and red-hot pincers by Dutch authorities later on. (For the Dutch side of this see *The Land and People of the Netherlands*.)

The Inquisition was most active against converted Jews between 1480 and 1530. There are no reliable statistics for the number of *conversos* tried or condemned during this period but it was certainly very large. One historian estimates that the Inquisition executed five thousand people in those fifty years, of whom between 80 to 90 percent were *conversos*. Another historian has recently referred to this as the "first holocaust." After 1530 the Inquisition turned its attention to the Catholic population as a whole. It focused on the clergy, especially for soliciting in the confessional, and policed unorthodox beliefs, blasphemy, superstition, and witchcraft and certain aspects of morality, such as bigamy. From 1540 to 1700 the Inquisition heard about 49,000 cases but passed only 500 death sentences.

Royal Power

The Inquisition was a powerful institution that was controlled by the crown. It was an important part of the efforts of Ferdinand and Isabella to reassert the power of the monarchy after the political conflicts that had ravaged both Castile and Aragon in the first half of the fifteenth century. The monarchs recovered royal land that had been given away earlier and created a more effective system of taxation. They reorganized the *hermandades*, local police forces that existed in the towns, and brought them under royal control. The aristocracy was kept in line by destroying feudal castles and limiting the power of the offices they held. Royal officials, known as *corregidores*, were sent to

Francisco Ricci de Guevara's painting The Act of Faith in the Plaza Mayor of Madrid, June 30, 1680, Presided Over by King Charles II.   Museo del Prado, Madrid

the towns to curb their autonomy. Ferdinand and Isabella persuaded Pope Innocent VIII (1484–1492) to allow them to nominate candidates for important ecclesiastical positions. Finally, they oversaw the reforms undertaken by Cardinal Ximénez de Cisneros, which left the Spanish church strengthened and in a position to effectively resist Protestantism. All in all, Ferdinand and Isabella left their kingdoms, and especially Castile, with a strong state. Spain would need all of that strength to face the challenges and opportunities that lay ahead.

1492

1492 was the most important year in the history of Spain, and also one of the most important in world history. By the middle of April Ferdinand and Isabella had completed the Reconquest, expelled the Jews from their kingdoms, and signed a contract with an Italian sailor named Christopher Columbus—Cristóbal Colón to the Spaniards—to undertake the voyage of exploration that initiated the permanent European occupation of the Americas.

The End of the Reconquest

The last remnant of Islamic Spain was the kingdom of Granada. The internal political conflicts in Castile protected the kingdom through most of the fifteenth century. That situation came to an end by 1480.

Ferdinand and Isabella had asserted royal authority once more, and in 1482 they began the assault on Granada. They naturally wanted to incorporate the last outstanding piece of territory on the peninsula into their kingdoms, but they were also driven, or at least Isabella was, by genuine religious conviction.

Ferdinand was less zealous than his wife and more of a political realist. He was also a brilliant diplomat; it is frequently said that he was the model for Machiavelli's *The Prince*, perhaps the most influential book on statecraft ever written. (See *The Land and People of Italy*.) His diplomatic skill was crucial in the war against Granada, for it allowed him to take advantage of a conflict over the succession to the throne there. Twice the Spaniards captured Boabdil, one of the claimants of the throne of the Moorish kingdom, and twice Boabdil put himself under the protection of Ferdinand and Isabella. However, when his rival was defeated by the Christians in 1489, Boabdil turned against the Spaniards. Throughout 1490 and 1491 Ferdinand and Isabella prepared to besiege the city of Granada, but in the end Boabdil surrendered. On January 2, 1492, Boabdil gave the keys of the Alhambra to Ferdinand. Four days later Ferdinand and Isabella entered Granada in triumph.

Ferdinand described that entry in a letter he sent to King Henry VII of England. The content of the letter was described by the contemporary English historian Francis Bacon.

. . . showing, amongst other things, that the king would not, by any means in person enter the city until he had first seen the Cross set up upon the greater tower of Granada, whereby it became Christian ground. That likewise, before he would enter, he did homage to God above, pronouncing by a herald from the height of that tower, that he did acknowledge to have recovered the kingdom by the help of God Almighty, and the glorious Virgin and the virtuous apostle Saint James, and the Holy Father Innocent VIII, together with the aids and services of his prelates, nobles and commons. That yet he stirred not from his camp till he had seen a little army of martyrs, to the number of seven hundred and more Christians, that had lived in bonds and servitude as slaves to the Moors, pass before his eyes, singing a psalm for their redemption; and that he had given tribute unto God, by arms and relief extended to them all, for his admission into the city.

From Reconquest to Conquest

With this victory the Reconquest was over; but it was soon replaced by conquest pure and simple. In 1494 Pope Alexander VI blessed the Castilians' desire to carry the struggle against Islam into Africa; three years later they captured the coastal town of Melilla. The offensive was resumed only in 1505, but Isabella had died the year before. The Archbishop of Toledo, Francisco Ximénez de Cisneros (1436–1517), continued to advocate an aggressive policy, but Ferdinand was much less interested in Africa than in Italy, where the Aragonese had a long history of involvement. Ferdinand's approach won out and in the end Spain did no more than establish a few garrisons on the coast of North Africa.

After the surrender of Granada the Moslem population was allowed to remain and was permitted to keep its customs and laws and even its own judges. Fearing a possible revolt, Ferdinand and Isabella encouraged the Moslem leaders to leave the country; Boabdil and some six thousand others did so.

So long as the Christian authorities allowed the Moslems to practice their religion in peace, there were no serious problems. In 1499, however, the policy of tolerance gave way to one of forced conversion. The much-feared revolt broke out almost immediately in the Alpujarras, part of the Sierra Nevada, a mountain range above Granada. Ferdinand personally put down the revolt, and the defeated Moslems were given the choice of converting or leaving the country. Most were poor and emigration was not a realistic option, so Spain was left with a large population of *moriscos*, nominal converts to Christianity who continued to practice their religion and customs despite decrees forbidding Islamic worship.

For sixty years the *moriscos* were left alone, but in 1567 the government decided that the laws banning the use of Arabic and Moslem clothing should be enforced. This caused a second revolt in the Alpujarras, which lasted from 1568 to 1570. The defeat of this revolt led to the expulsion of eighty thousand *moriscos* from Granada to Castile. They were replaced by settlers brought in from northern Spain.

Resented by their new Christian neighbors for their religion, their industriousness, and their numbers, the *moriscos* remained a distinct society in the heart of Catholic Spain. Finally, in 1609, they were expelled to northern Africa. Some 275,000 of the 300,000 *moriscos* left. About half had lived in Aragon, where they represented about one sixth of the population, and Valencia, where they accounted for one third. These regions could not afford such a human loss, and their economies suffered.

The elites, especially the Valencian nobility on whose lands they lived, did their best to protect the *moriscos*. The hatred came from the poorer elements of Christian society, who had to compete with them. This hatred was expressed in charges of tightfistedness and immorality. These were described by Miguel de Cervantes in "The Dogs' Colloquium," one of his *Exemplary Novels*, published in 1613.

It would be a miracle to find among so many people even one who believes sincerely in the sacred Christian faith. Their sole aim is to coin money and then keep it, and in order to gain work they do not eat. When a *real* enters into their possession . . . they condemn it to perpetual imprisonment and eternal obscurity; so that always gaining and never spending, they accumulate the greater part of the money that there is in Spain. They are its money-bags, its moth, its magpies and its weasels. They gather everything, they hide everything, and they swallow everything. There is no chastity among them, and neither men nor women enter the religious life. They all of them marry, they all multiply, because sober living augments the causes of generation. War does not consume them, nor any occupation overtask them. They rob us quietly and easily, and with the fruits of our inheritance which they resell to us they wax rich.

These and other similar stereotypes were not limited to sixteenth-century Spain: They have been repeatedly used against ethnic minorities and are still current in North America today.

The Expulsion of the Jews

The other religious minority did not last nearly so long. Less than three months after the completion of the Reconquest, on March 31, 1492, Ferdinand and Isabella expelled the Jews from all lands belonging to the crowns of Castile and Aragon.

Religious tolerance had never been a virtue in Christian Europe, and the situation of *convivencia* in medieval Spain had been very much an exception. One threat posed by the Jews was the temptation—or encouragement—they provided to the *conversos* to return to their original religion. That is, they contributed to apostasy. But this was not only a religious threat. In the eyes of European monarchs, whose right to rule came from God as confirmed by the church, religious unity was the essential basis of political unity. This was the principal reason Catholic rulers would struggle so long and hard against Protestantism in the sixteenth century.

The expulsion was the logical culmination of the reduction of reli-

The Morisco *Voice*

The *moriscos* produced a substantial but little-known literature. Known as Aljamiado literature, it was written in Castilian but using Arabic script, similar to the Ladino, a Spanish dialect written in Hebrew script, used by Spanish Jews. The most famous Aljamiado writer was the sixteenth-century poet Muhammad Rabadan. He was born in Aragon but lived much of his life in Tunis. The following verses lament the state of the *moriscos* in Spain, which is presented as divine punishment:

> *God made possible*
> *That the Moors of this kingdom*
> *With so many persecutions*
> *Would be punished and enslaved.*
> *Having lost the books*

gious tolerance that had been going on for a century. Ferdinand and Isabella had already expelled Jews from specific parts of their realms, such as Seville. The Edict of Expulsion was formally decreed at the end of April. All Jews were to be out of the country by the end of July. The most common estimate for the number who left is 160,000 but there are no reliable statistics, and historians now think that the number may have been much smaller. Those who did not emigrate converted to Catholicism. These last-minute converts included leading members of the Jewish community and holders of important government offices, such as Abraham Senior. Some went to North Africa and

Without leaving a trace;
Scholars are gone
Some dead, others jailed
The Inquisition rampant
With great force and pressures,
Implementing with rigor
Cruelty and excesses;
Almost everywhere
The earth is made to tremble:
They apprehend here and there
The newly baptized,
Imposing on them every day
Galleys, torment and fire
Along with other calamities
For which God alone knows the secret.

Italy. The vast majority of the Jews went to Portugal, but they were expelled from there four years later when King Emmanuel I married the daughter of Ferdinand and Isabella. Many finally ended up in Holland.

The expulsion of the Jews is an important ingredient in Spain's reputation for intolerance. Yet this act was only typical of a Christian Europe that had seen the Jews expelled from one country after another. England in 1290, France in 1391, and a large number of places in the Holy Roman Empire in the fifteenth century, beginning with Prague in 1400, had all expelled their Jews long before Spain did.

Even so, the expulsion from Spain has a special place in Jewish his-

The Edict of Expulsion

As we have been informed that in our kingdoms there are some bad Christians, who follow Jewish practices and apostatize from our holy Catholic faith, much of which was caused by communication between Jews and Christians. . . . The contact which Christians continue to have with Jews, who lose no opportunity to seduce loyal Christians from our faith and pervert their beliefs, teaching them the ceremonies and observances of their faith . . . and trying to circumcise them and their sons . . . all of which is proved by the many confessions of the Jews themselves as well as of those who were deceived by them and which has caused much harm to our holy Catholic faith. . . .

Therefore, having consulted with some prelates and nobles and other learned members of our Council and after much deliberation, we order that all Jews leave our kingdoms and never return to them. . . . By the end of July of this year all Jews, and their children and their Jewish servants and family members, of all ages, must leave our kingdoms and not return to them on pain of death and confiscation of all their goods . . . without the right to any trial. And no person in our kingdoms, whatever their condition, should take in any Jew after the end of July.

And so that until the end of July the Jews may better dispose of their belongings we take them under our royal protection and assure that they may move about and freely and voluntarily dispose of their goods, and that during this time no one do them harm. And we allow the Jews to take with them all their belongings except gold or coins. . . .

tory. Spain had been home to a large Jewish population that had flourished both culturally and economically. Many Sephardi (from Sefarad,
the Jewish name for Spain) have kept Ladino, their version of the
Spanish language, alive for five centuries. Some still retain the keys to
the houses owned by their ancestors in Spain.

America

In 1486 Christopher Columbus, the son of an obscure weaver from the
Italian city of Genoa, proposed to Ferdinand and Isabella his project of
reaching Asia by sailing west across the Atlantic Ocean, or the Ocean
Sea, as it was then called. The Spanish monarchs were his last chance,
as he had already failed to interest the kings of Portugal and France.

Why did Columbus think that anyone would be the least interested in such a plan? Since 1453, when the Turks had captured
Constantinople and cut the overland trade route that brought Asian
spices to Europe, Europeans had been seeking a sea route to replace it.
Even before that they had been looking for sources of slaves and new
fishing grounds. Portugal played the leading role in these voyages of
exploration, which took the Portuguese south along the coast of Africa,
to the Atlantic islands—Madeira, the Azores, the Cape Verdes, and the
Canaries—and, in 1488, around the Cape of Good Hope.

Isabella was intrigued by Columbus's idea from the first but Ferdinand was less convinced, and in any case, the war against Granada
was still going on. For six years Columbus persisted in his attempts to
win their support. He also put together a group of financial backers
that included Ferdinand's treasurer, Luís de Santangel, the Duke of
Medinaceli, and some Genoese bankers who loaned money to the
monarchs. Finally, in January 1492, only a few days after the surrender
of Granada, Isabella decided to sponsor Columbus's voyage, even

though two royal commissions had found the sailor's ideas impractical.

Columbus wanted to prove his geographic theory that one could go east by sailing west, but he was no disinterested scholar. He also wanted rewards, and it was only in April, after much hard bargaining, that the contract under which he undertook his voyage was signed. This contract, known as a *capitulación*, was similar to those Spanish rulers had signed with military leaders during the Reconquest, granting them proper rewards while guaranteeing the rights and power of the Crown in the conquered lands.

Columbus's Contract with Ferdinand and Isabella, April 17, 1492

The following are the favors which, on the petition of Don Christopher Columbus, Your Highnesses grant him as reward for his discoveries in the Ocean Seas and for the voyage that with God's help he is now about to make in Your Highnesses' service.

First, Your Highnesses, as Sovereigns of the said Ocean Seas, appoint the said Christopher Columbus, now and henceforth, their Admiral in all islands and mainlands that shall be discovered by his effort and diligence in the said Ocean Seas, for the duration of his life, and after his death, his heirs and successors in perpetuity, with all the rights and privileges belonging to that office. . . .

Your highnesses also appoint the said Don Christopher their Viceroy and Governor General in all islands and mainlands that . . . he may discover and acquire in the said Seas. For the government of each of them he may nominate three candidates for each office, and Your Highnesses shall select the man best qualified for their service, so that the lands that Our Lord permits him to discover and acquire in Your Highnesses' service may be the better governed.

Your Highnesses grant to the said Don Christopher Columbus one tenth of all merchandise, whether pearls, gems, gold, silver, spices, or goods of any kind that may be acquired by purchase, barter, or any other means, within the boundaries of the said Admiralty jurisdiction. After all the expenses have been deducted, of what remains he may take and keep the tenth part and dispose of it as he pleases, the other nine parts to accrue to Your Highnesses.

In all vessels fitted out for the said trade at any time the said Don Christopher Columbus may, if he wishes, invest one eighth of the total cost of the fitting-out and may keep for himself one eighth of the profit of the venture.

I the King   I the Queen

Columbus left Palos de la Frontera with his three ships, the *Niña*, the *Pinta*, and the *Santa María*, on August 3, 1492. They stopped in the Canary Islands and spent four weeks loading supplies before setting sail again on September 8. The ships were then at sea for more than a month without sighting land. Both Columbus and his crew became discouraged. On October 10 he noted in his journal that the crew "would endure no more." In the first hours of the morning on October 12 land was finally sighted.

Columbus called the island where he landed San Salvador. (This island is believed to have been Watling Island, today part of the Bahamas, but there is some controversy over this.) The island was not in Asia or anywhere near it, but Columbus never accepted this. He went to his grave believing the islands where he landed on his first and three subsequent voyages lay just off the Asian mainland.

Whatever Columbus might have thought he had done, he had not "discovered" anything. If America was the "New World," it was only new to the Europeans. After all, there were millions of people living in the Americas—or the Indies, as the Spaniards called them—when Columbus arrived. To talk about the "discovery" of America is to as-

Columbus's First Day in America

From *Journal of Christopher Columbus*:

Thursday October 11/ Two hours after midnight land appeared, at a distance about two leagues from them. They took in all sail, remaining with the mainsail . . . and kept jogging, waiting for a day, Friday, on which they reached the small island of the Lucayos, which is called in the language of the Indians "Guanahani." Immediately they saw naked people, and the admiral went ashore in the armed boat, and Martín Alonso Pinzón and Vicente Yáñez, his brother, who was captain of the *Niña*. The admiral brought out the royal standard, and the captains went with the two banners of the Green Cross, which the admiral flew on all the ships as a flag, with an F and a Y [for Ferdinand and Isabella] and over each letter their crown. . . . When they had landed they saw very green trees and much water and fruit of various kinds. The admiral called the two captains and the others who had landed . . . and said that they should bear witness and testimony how he, before them all, took possession of the island, as in fact he did, for the King and Queen his sovereigns, making the declarations which were required. . . . Soon many people of the island gathered there. What follows are the actual words of the admiral. . . .

"I, in order that they might feel great amity towards us, because I knew they were a people to be delivered and converted to our holy faith by love rather than by force, gave to some among them red caps and glass beads, which they hung round their necks, and many other things of little value. At this they were greatly pleased and became so entirely our friends that it was a wonder to see. Afterwards they came swimming to the ships' boats, where we were, and brought us parrots and cotton thread in balls, and spears and many other things, and we exchanged for them other things, such as small glass beads and hawks' bells, which we gave to them. In fact, they took all and gave all, such as they had, with good will, but it seemed to me that they were a people very deficient in everything. They all go naked as their mothers bore them, and the women also, although I saw only one very young girl. And all those whom I did see were youths, so that I did not see one who was over thirty years of age; they were very well built, with very handsome bodies and very good faces. Their hair is coarse, almost like the hairs of a horse's tail, and short; they wear their hair down over their eyebrows, except for a few strands behind, which they wear long and they never cut. Some of them are painted black and they are the color of the people of the Canaries, neither black nor white, and some of them are painted white and some red and some in any color they can find. Some of them paint their faces, some their whole bodies, some only the eyes, and some only the nose. They do not bear arms or know them, for I showed them swords and they took them by the blade and cut themselves out of ignorance. They have no iron. Their spears are certain reeds, without iron, and some of these have a fish tooth at the end, while others are pointed in various ways. They are all generally fairly tall, good looking and well proportioned. I saw some who bore marks of wounds on their bodies, and I made signs to ask them how this came about, and they indicated to me that came people from other islands, which are near, and wished to capture them, and they defended themselves. . . . They should be good servants and of quick intelligence, since I see that they very soon say all that is said to them, and I believe that they would easily be made Christians, for it appeared to me that they had no creed. Our Lord willing, at the time of my departure I will bring back six of them to Your Highnesses, that they may learn to talk. I saw no beast of any kind in this island, except parrots."

Engraving of Columbus landing on the island of Hispaniola, taken from the edition of Columbus's Letter to Gabriel Sánchez *published in Basel, Switzerland, 1493.*

sume that it is only the arrival of the Europeans that gives a land any importance and that the indigenous inhabitants have no significance of their own.

Columbus was not even the first European to reach America; the Vikings had done so centuries before. But the Viking presence in America was brief and left no lasting impression, either there or in Europe. Columbus brought the Europeans to stay, with incalculable consequences for both the "Old World" and the "New."

Imperial Spain

For almost eight hundred years Spaniards' attention and energies were dominated by the Reconquest. They were in touch with the rest of Christian Europe, but internal affairs were their primary concern.

This changed dramatically after 1492. Columbus opened a "new world" to Spain, and within forty years of his first voyage Castile had become the ruler of an empire that reached into the Americas and Asia. Spain's American empire was important, but its future was determined much more by its sudden and unexpected arrival at the very center of European affairs.

The Habsburg Connection

Spain's new position was the result of the complexities of the diplomacy of Ferdinand of Aragon. His main concern was to protect Aragonese holdings in Italy against France; his principal weapons were dynastic marriages. He arranged marriages for his children with those of other rulers with whom he wanted to establish alliances. One daughter, Catherine of Aragon, was first married to Arthur, heir to the English throne, and after his death she became the first wife of Henry VIII. Another daughter, Isabella, was married to Prince Alfonso of Portugal. When he died she married King Emmanuel of Portugal, and when she died Emmanuel married her sister, María. Finally, the Catholic King's only son, Juan, married Margaret, the daughter of the Holy Roman Emperor Maximilian I. Juan's sister Juana married the Emperor's son, Philip of Burgundy. "Holy Roman Empire" was the name given to a number of principalities and other small states in what are now Germany, Austria, Czechoslovakia, and even parts of Italy and France. By this time the emperor was habitually selected from the Habsburg family, which ruled Austria.

Spanish Rulers, 1474–1700

Isabella of Castile	1474–1504
Ferdinand of Aragon	1479–1516
Juana of Castile ("the Mad")	1504–1555
Charles I	1516–1556
Philip II	1556–1598
Philip III	1598–1621
Philip IV	1621–1665
Charles II	1665–1700

The Spanish Royal House in the Fifteenth and Sixteenth Centuries

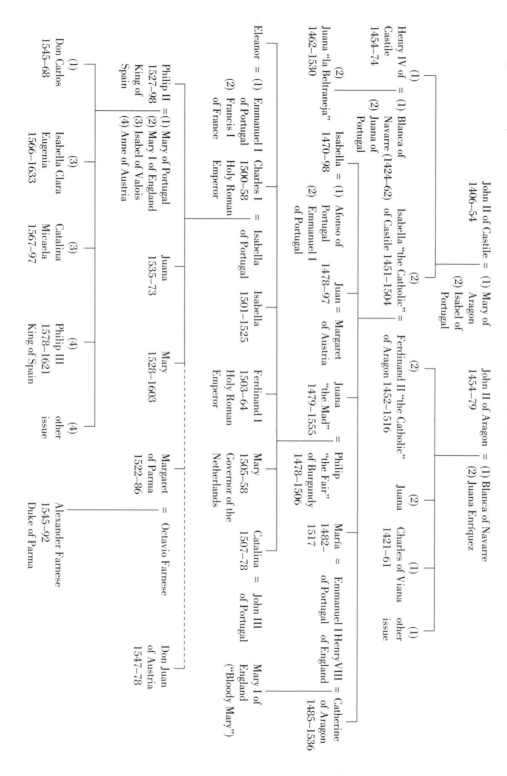

These marriages were designed to realize two goals. The first was to establish a Spanish claim to the throne of Portugal. This Ferdinand did successfully, and in 1580 his great-grandson, Philip II, became King of Portugal. The second goal was to create an alliance with England and the Holy Roman Empire that would isolate France. Here Ferdinand had less success.

The most important outcome of all these marriages was one Ferdinand neither expected nor wanted. The death of Prince Juan, the heir to the throne, and then of Juan's oldest sister, Isabella of Portugal, and of her son Miguel, meant that the crowns of Castile and Aragon passed to Juana. But Juana was mentally unstable, and when her husband died suddenly in 1506, she went mad and retired to Tordesillas, accompanied by her husband's corpse. She spent the remaining forty-six years of her life there. This left her six-year-old son, Charles of Ghent, as heir to the throne.

Charles the Fifth and First

Charles became King when Ferdinand died in 1516. He arrived in Spain the next year. Spain was only one of Charles' many inheritances. From his paternal grandfather, Maximilian, he received Austria; from his paternal grandmother, Mary of Burgundy, he received the Low Countries, today Holland and Belgium. In addition, in 1519 he became Holy Roman Emperor, as Charles V. In Spain, though, he was known as Charles I. The imperial title brought more prestige than real power. The emperor was elected by the princes who ruled the various states that made up Germany. No Spanish ruler had held this office, although Alfonso X of Castile had spent vast sums of money trying to influence the voters.

Charles did not get off to a good start in Spain. To many Spaniards he was a young, ugly foreigner who could not even speak Spanish. He was also surrounded by foreign advisers who appeared to be interested in little besides enriching themselves at Spanish expense. Following his election as Holy Roman Emperor Charles prepared to leave for Germany. As part of his preparations he summoned the Cortes of Castile to grant him money. The Cortes was an assembly of the clergy, the nobility, and the common people. These three groupings were the "estates" into which Spanish society, as well as society in most of medieval and early modern Europe, was divided. Together they had to approve the monarch's requests for funds. By the end of the fifteenth century, however, the clergy and nobility rarely participated, and the delegates came almost entirely from the eighteen Castilian towns entitled to representation. A number of the towns resisted Charles' demands, and when he set sail in May 1520 they rose in revolt.

The rebels, who were known as the *Comuneros*, were driven by resentment of the foreigners surrounding Charles and what they saw as his excessive and illegal demands for money. Even though the rebels were divided among themselves, especially by popular hatred of the aristocracy, it was almost a year before the revolt was finally put down, in April 1521.

Spain at War

Between 1520 and 1665 Spain was almost continually at war in one place or another. At times fighting raged on two or even three fronts. Virtually all these wars were defensive, attempts by Spanish rulers to preserve their possessions against foreign aggression or internal revolt. Spanish rulers did not fight wars to conquer new territory in Europe. In a number of cases, such as Charles V's wars against the Protestants in Germany or Philip II's struggle against the Ottoman Empire in the

Equestrian portrait of Charles V painted by Titian in commemoration of the King's victory over the Protestants in August 1547.   Museo del Prado, Madrid

Charles V on the Difficulties of Ruling

In 1543 Charles set off from Spain once again to fight a war, this time in Germany. He named his sixteen-year-old son, Philip, as regent. Before leaving, he sent Philip a long letter offering advice. Much of the letter analyzed the personalities and ambitions of the leading people at court. Of the Duke of Alba he wrote that he was "the ablest statesman and soldier I have. Consult him, in military affairs above all, but do not depend on him entirely in these or any other matters. The great nobles will be too happy to secure your favor and through you govern the land, but if you are governed in this way it will be your ruin."

Charles' letter is striking less for its political insight than for the sense of disappointment and sadness it conveys. It is as if he already knew that he would not realize his ambitions and that there was little of use he could tell his son. He sounds a truly humble man, not the mighty ruler.

On the whole I will admit that I have much reason to be satisfied with your behavior, but I would have you perfect and to speak frankly, you have some things to improve yet. Your confessor is your old teacher. . . . He is a good man but I hope he will take better care of your conscience than he did of your studies. . . .

It is a great trouble and concern to me that I have to leave you my Empire in such a state of need and I do not know how we shall all survive. All things are in God's hand. . . . I ought to tell you more, my son, only the really important things are so obscure and full of doubt that I can not give you definite advice. I am myself still undetermined and largely unenlightened. Indeed it is one of the main objects of my journey to see clearly what has to be done. Trust in the will of God and let all else alone.

Mediterranean, religious motives were prominent. But no Spanish ruler put the defense of Catholicism ahead of his own imperial interests.

Charles V fought wars against France in the 1520's and 1530's for control of Italy, and he also fought the Barbary pirates, Moslems based in Tunis and Algiers who threatened Spanish and Genoese shipping in the Mediterranean. But his principal problem was Protestantism. This was a religious threat to the Catholic Church but, more important for Charles, it was a direct threat to his position in Germany. Although Charles won a number of military victories over the German princes who had adopted Protestantism, he was unable to find a military solution for this religious problem. By the 1550's he was losing ground in Germany and was forced to recognize the status of Protestantism there.

In 1555 and 1556 Charles abdicated as ruler of his various possessions and retired to the monastery of Yuste, in western Spain, where he died in 1558. In his abdication he recognized the failure of his attempt to keep his inheritance intact and Catholic, which had been his life's work. He divided his possessions into two parts, leaving each to a different heir. His brother Ferdinand received Austria and the Holy Roman Empire; his son Philip received Castile and its American empire, Aragon and its possessions in Italy, and the Low Countries.

"Let Each One Perform What Has Been Allotted Him"

The abiding image of Philip II, in his own time as well as later, is of a cold and fully controlled man, unemotional in either victory or defeat. There is something to this. In 1541, following the defeat of Charles V's expedition to Algiers, Philip wrote to his father:

Consider that returning from difficult enterprises without victory does not rob kings and great commanders of the merit of their valor. The one who loses by force of fortune ought to be more consoled since against his prudence and greatness all the elements conspired. It is never good to trouble oneself over events: let each one perform what has been allotted him, for if he ordained things well, he labored successfully.

Almost fifty years later, after the defeat of the great Armada, he expressed similar sentiments in a letter to the bishops of Spain:

The uncertainties of naval enterprises are well known and the fate which has befallen the Armada bears this out. . . . I give thanks to God for the mercy He has shown. In the storms through which the Armada sailed, it might have suffered a worse fate and if it did not must be attributed to the many prayers for its success.

Philip was also known as being a very hard-working King. In 1587 Girolamo Lippomano, the Venetian ambassador in Madrid, filed this report on Philip's work habits:

His Majesty . . . attends assiduously to affairs, though he is . . . averse to public audiences. . . . He is never idle, for besides his wish to read for himself all the correspondence which passes between his ambassadors and governors in all parts of his great domains . . . he writes every day with his own hand . . . minutes, opinions and orders which are transmitted to his [officials]; and it is hardly to be believed how much time he spends in signing letters, licenses, patents and other affairs of grace and justice, which on certain days amount to two thousand. . . .

Despite his reduced inheritance Philip's reign was even more filled with warfare than his father's had been. Philip had to face some new dangers. For almost twenty years his main problem lay in the Mediterranean, where the Turks under Suleiman the Magnificent had expanded their empire. Then, at the battle of Lepanto in October 1571, Spain, together with Venice and the Papacy, was able to stop the Turkish advance.

Revolt   Philip II's greatest difficulty, though, was not the Turks but the revolt in what is today the Netherlands, which began in 1566. The motives for the revolt were a combination of religious dissent, as Protestantism spread rapidly through the Netherlands, and opposition to Philip's attempts to reorganize the Church and government structure while imposing heavier taxes. (See *The Land and People of the Netherlands.*) Spain committed tremendous resources to its campaigns in the Low Countries but was unable to suppress the revolt in Philip's lifetime. The conflict in the Netherlands remained a running sore for both his son and his grandson.

Pirates   A final problem came from British piracy in America. Captains such as John Hawkins and Francis Drake preyed on Spanish shipping from the 1570's on, although at first they were little more than an annoyance. By the 1580's Philip II had decided that the best way to deal with English pirates was to strike at England itself. His determination to pursue the "enterprise of England" was reinforced after England became directly involved in the Netherlands after 1585.

Invasion

Philip himself directed the planning of the invasion of England. He even ordered that the sailors should neither swear nor gamble! A fleet sailing from Lisbon was to meet a military force from the Low Countries and protect it while it crossed the English Channel in barges. The Armada, comprising 130 ships, 2,431 artillery pieces, and 27,000 men, left Lisbon in May 1588 and entered the English Channel on July 30. Despite constant English attacks the Spanish fleet progressed steadily for six days, but then, at the crucial moment, everything fell apart. The Spanish commander in the Low Countries,

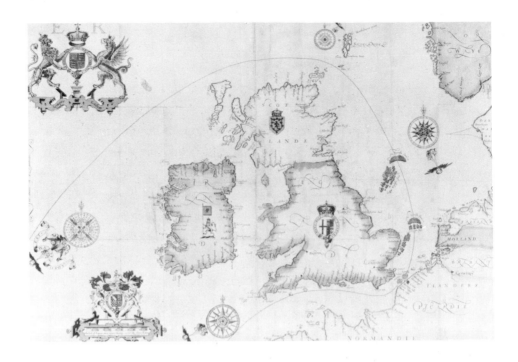

Contemporary map showing the route of the Spanish Armada around the British Isles.
British Museum, London

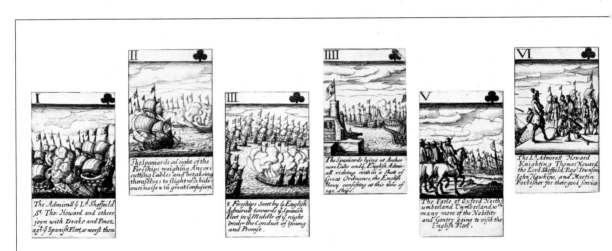

Six English playing cards from a deck with scenes from the Spanish attempt to invade England. National Maritime Museum, Greenwich, England

Alexander Farnese, did not have appropriate ships to provide cover for his barges, something about which he had warned Philip. He decided not to send his army to meet the Armada. On August 7 and 8 the English used fire ships to break up the Armada and then attacked successfully. The commander of the Armada, the Duke of Medina Sidonia, was able to re-form his fleet, but bad weather took over and drove it north around Scotland and then westward around the coast of Ireland. The remnants of the Armada reached Spain at the end of September.

Despite this defeat Spain continued to control the Atlantic crossing, and in the 1590's it improved its security measures for the crossing as well as its defenses in America itself. Philip was even able to send a second Armada, almost as large as the first, against England in 1597, but it too was scattered by a storm in the Channel.

The reign of Philip III (ruled 1598–1621) was considerably more peaceful. He made peace with England in 1604 and then, in 1609, he signed the Twelve Years' Truce with the United Provinces. But his successor, Philip IV (ruled 1621–1665), returned to a policy of multiple military commitments in an attempt to protect his possessions. Spain was almost always at war somewhere throughout the 45 years of Philip IV's reign.

The Court of Philip IV

The Spanish court was the most formal in Europe. All the ceremonies and functions were laid out in minute detail in written documents known as *etiquetas*.

The king's life was both extremely public and extremely private. He was presented "to the world" on certain, specific occasions, but for the rest he was rarely seen in public. Once a week he ate a ceremonial meal in public, but he took his other meals alone. The queen also ate alone, in her own separate household.

The Fate of the Armada

One of the Spanish ships, *El Gran Grifón*, was caught up in storms around the Orkney Islands, off Scotland. A member of the crew described their situation:

> We were fit only to die, for the wind was so strong and the sea so wild that the waves mounted to the skies, knocking the ship about so that all the men were exhausted, and yet unable to keep down the water that leaked through our gaping seams. . . . The poor soldiers too, who had worked incessantly at the pumps and buckets, lost heart and let the water rise. . . . So we gave way to despair and called upon the Virgin Mary to be our intermediary in so bitter a pass; and we looked towards the land with full eyes and hearts.

The ship did reach land, an island only three miles long. According to one survivor,

> We found the island peopled by seventeen households in huts, more like hovels than anything else. They are savage people, whose usual food is fish, without bread, except for a few barley-meal bannocks cooked over the embers of a fuel . . . which they extract from the earth and call turf. . . . They are a very dirty people, neither Christians, nor altogether heretics. It is true they confess the doc-

The court was most spectacular during the reign of Philip IV, whose advisers worked hard to make him the "planet King" who "illuminates distant hemispheres." There were many public spectacles; one of Philip's favorites was the *juego de caña*, a kind of joust. The Earl of Clarendon, who visited Madrid in 1649, described the one he saw:

trine [Calvinism] that once a year is preached to them by people sent from another island . . . is not good, but they say they dare not contradict it, which is a pity.

These survivors and those from other ships, some six hundred men in all, were eventually taken to the Scottish mainland. Most were sent back to Spain months later.

The Duke of Medina Sidonia and his flagship reached Spain in late September. The Duke described the disastrous situation in a letter to the King, and did not spare himself the blame.

> The troubles and miseries we have suffered cannot be described to Your Majesty. . . . On board some of the ships that are in there has not been a drop of water to drink for a fortnight. On my own ship, a hundred and eighty men have died of sickness . . . and all the rest of the people on board are ill, many of typhus and other infectious diseases. All sixty of the men of my own household have either died or fallen sick, and only two remain able to serve me. Great as the miseries have been, we are now worse off than ever, for the men are ill and the little biscuit and wine we have left will be finished in a week. We are therefore in a wretched state, and I implore Your Majesty to send some money quickly to buy some necessities. . . . Everything is in disorder, and must at once be put in competent hands. . . .

[It was] an exercise . . . performed by squadrons of horse seeming to charge each other with great fierceness, with bucklers in their left hands, and a kind of cane in their right, which, when they come within little more than a horse-length, they throw with all the strength they can, and . . . as soon as they have thrown their darts, they wheel about in a full gallop, till they can turn to receive the assault from those whom they had charged; and so several

The pantheon of the kings in the Escorial Palace built during the reign of Philip II. On the left are the caskets of Charles V, Philip II, Philip III, and Philip IV. Courtesy of the Tourist Office of Spain

squadrons of twenty or five-and-twenty horse run round and charge each other . . . the horses are very beautiful and well adorned; the men richly clad and must be good horsemen, otherwise they could not obey the quick motion and turn of their horses.

There was a short war with France in Italy from 1627 to 1631 and then, from 1635 to 1659, there was continual warfare between the two countries on various fronts. The struggle in the Low Countries resumed in 1621, and in order to maintain the supply route from Italy, Spain became involved in the Thirty Years' War in Germany. In 1640 both Portugal, which had become part of the Spanish monarchy in 1580, and Catalonia rebelled against Philip's rule. When the war with France ended in 1659, Philip almost immediately declared war on Portugal.

Spain and the Empire

Throughout almost 150 years of protracted warfare Spain continued to rule a vast empire. However, the nature of that empire prevented Spanish rulers from using all its resources easily. Charles I and the three Philips did not rule a single, highly centralized, and integrated political unit but a grab bag of territories, each of which retained its own laws and institutions and which were united only in the person of the monarch.

This was true even in Spain itself. Castile and Aragon each retained its distinct personality. Only in Castile did Spanish monarchs rule absolutely, although even there the Basque Provinces had a special status regarding taxes and military service. In Aragon the king was subject to the *fueros*, local laws which gave the Cortes the right to make laws and determine taxes. Spain's possessions in Italy—Sicily, Naples, and Milan—had their own institutions, as did the Low Countries and Portugal (which during the sixty years from 1580 to 1640 was ruled by Spanish kings).

Bankrupt

The cost of Spanish foreign policy was borne overwhelmingly by that part of the empire that could be taxed most easily, Castile. And that foreign policy was expensive. By the 1560's 84 percent of all the Crown's revenues in Castile were spent on warfare; by 1634 the figure had risen to 94 percent. New taxes were constantly imposed, and beginning with Philip III copper coins replaced silver. Even so, in many years revenues amounted to only half of expenditures, and the Crown had to borrow money from German and Genoese bankers at increasingly stiff interest rates. But even this was not enough, and Spanish kings had to declare bankruptcy in 1557, 1575, 1596, 1607, 1627, 1647, and 1653.

For Castile this was a disaster. The Castilian economy was not a particularly advanced one at the best of times, depending on the export of raw materials, especially wool. The effort to sustain a vast empire against numerous enemies for almost 150 years drained Castile of its economic energies.

The seventeenth century was a time of general crisis in Europe, but in Castile the crisis was more severe and prolonged than anywhere else. The starkest evidence is population, which fell from 8.4 million in 1590 to 7.5 million in 1717. Epidemics, famine, and war were the main causes. The continual increase in the weight of taxation that bore down on ordinary Castilians further undermined the economy. Manufacturing collapsed; textile cities such as Toledo and Segovia lost two thirds of their population in the century after 1590. Peasants could expect to pay as much as 50 percent of their crops to the state, the Church, and their landlords. Many abandoned agriculture for the cities and many villages became ghost towns.

The Crisis of Castile

The crisis of Castile was no secret. The government received large numbers of official and private reports on the subject. These were consistent in describing the misery that led to the depopulation of the countryside and the increasing number of beggars and transients. They were also consistent in pointing to war and especially taxation as the main culprits. Here is one example from Granada in 1621:

Numerous places have become depopulated and disappeared from the map, in some provinces as many as 50 or 60, their churches decayed, houses in ruins, property wasted and fields uncultivated. The vassals who formerly cultivated them now wander the roads with wives and children, searching from district to district for a living and eating herbs and roots to keep alive. Others go to distant provinces which are not so burdened with taxation . . . for it is the weight of taxation and the oppression of the tax collectors which are the principal causes of this depopulation.

At the beginning of the seventeenth century, it was already clear that Castile could not carry the burden of Spain's imperial defense alone and some attempts were made to get other parts of the empire, and especially Aragon and Catalonia, to contribute more generously. The most ambitious of these projects was proposed by Philip IV's chief minister, the Count-Duke of Olivares, who wanted to create a more united Spanish monarchy in which all the parts would contribute money and men to a central pool. As it turned out, Valencia gave less money than Olivares wanted and Catalonia refused outright, insisting on its right to provide soldiers to fight only inside Catalonia itself. Portugal, which had become part of the Spanish monarchy when Philip II inherited the crown in 1580, also refused.

The prolonged pressure to support the empire led to revolts in Catalonia and Portugal in 1640. The Portuguese were able to reestablish their independence, although Spain tried to reconquer Portugal until 1668. The Catalonians called on the French for protection, but the capital, Barcelona, was retaken in 1652, and most of the rest of Catalonia was returned to Spain in the Peace of the Pyrenees in 1659.

Conquistadores

One part of the empire where Spanish kings were not bound by local privileges or local institutions was America. Only forty years after Columbus' arrival, Spanish adventurers, the *conquistadores*, had added most of the American continent to the Spanish empire. They controlled lands from what are now the states of California, Arizona, New Mexico, and Texas south to Cape Horn. The conquest included the subjugation of two powerful and sophisticated empires: the Aztecs of Mexico, who were conquered by Hernán Cortés (1485–1547) in 1521, and the Incas of Peru, who were conquered by Francisco Pizarro (1476–1541) in 1532.

The new continental empire was a windfall. The Crown received one fifth of all gold and silver mined in America, and this gave Spanish kings more freedom to carry out their foreign policy. Nevertheless, as important as this American treasure was, it was never the basis of Spanish power, accounting for perhaps 10 percent of royal income.

Such large amounts of treasure needed protection as they were carried across the ocean. Spain was very successful in providing this protection through a system of convoys known as the *flota*. One fleet left

Spain for Vera Cruz, Mexico, the other for Portobello in Panama. For the return voyage they met up in Havana and crossed the Atlantic together. This system was directed against the pirates and privateers who swarmed over the Caribbean Sea. The *flota* system worked well, and very little treasure actually fell into the hands of pirates. Only twice in 150 years did the system fail seriously: In 1628 the Dutch admiral Piet Heyn captured the Mexican fleet off Cuba, and in 1656–1657 the English almost totally destroyed the Mexican fleet in the Canary Islands. Caribbean storms always presented a much greater danger.

In other respects Spain did not exploit the possibilities of the new empire as well as it might have. The colonies offered a growing market for Spanish products, but here Spain fell short. Colonial trade was organized into a monopoly based in Seville, but in the second half of the sixteenth century Spain was increasingly unable to meet colonial demand with its own products, and thus foreigners penetrated the monopoly. As a result, much of the silver that entered Spain left it just as quickly to pay for these goods. Much of the rest went straight into the hands of the Crown's foreign bankers.

Spain and America moved even further apart in the seventeenth century. Silver receipts began to decline around 1610 and never recovered. By 1660 the Crown was receiving only one fourteenth of what it received at the beginning of the century. At the same time the economies of the colonies were developing and coming to have less need of Spain. Castile could not provide the more sophisticated consumer goods the wealthy colonial elite wanted. These goods were provided by the Dutch, the French, and the British. Privately owned silver was increasingly invested in the colonies themselves. Shipbuilding became a major industry, and by 1640 more of the ships used in the transatlantic trade were built in America than in Spain. Economically, the American colonies were already largely independent.

In the old central district of Barcelona a sculptor makes religious images for churches.
Sergio Purtell

Religion

Religion was an important issue in many of the wars Spain fought in the sixteenth and seventeenth centuries. The Reformation, which began in 1517 when Martin Luther denounced abuses within the Catholic Church and certain central features of Catholic belief, produced a split in European Christianity and led to the emergence of a number of new churches, collectively known as Protestant. These new religions spread rapidly in parts of Germany and the Low Countries and represented a threat to Habsburg rule.

Protestantism never made much headway in Spain itself. In large part this was because many of the abuses attacked by Luther did not exist in the Spanish Church, which had been reformed during the reign of Ferdinand and Isabella. And the Inquisition still existed to keep anyone who took an interest in religious dissent in line.

The new religious climate of the sixteenth century seemed to stimulate Spanish Catholicism. Spanish theologians played a significant role at the Council of Trent (1545–1563), where the Catholic Church developed its response to the Protestant challenge. A new religious order devoted to missionary work and with a special vow of obedience to the Pope, the Jesuits, was founded in 1534 by Saint Ignatius Loyola (1491–1556), a Spanish Basque by birth.

Mysticism, the experience of an individual making direct contact with the divine, was an important feature of Spanish Catholicism at this time, and the outstanding figure was Saint Teresa of Avila (1515–1582). She came from a family of *conversos*, Jews who had converted to Catholicism, and one of her grandfathers went before the Inquisition and was forced to do penance for having returned to Jewish practices. At nineteen she became a Carmelite nun and later founded a number of convents of reformed Carmelites. She also wrote a number of

Giant statues are carried through the streets as part of local religious festivals.
Corina Iaizzo

books, among them a spiritual autobiography, an account of the founding of her convents, and spiritual guides. Much of the power of her writing comes from her use of down-to-earth, and at times erotic, imagery to convey the feeling of the mystical experience.

Not all religious activity was directed to ends so elevated as spiritual fulfillment. Besides the official beliefs of the Church, and frequently criticized by Church authorities, there was a local religion of sacred places, relics, local patron saints, processions, vows, and unusual ceremonies. This was the religion of most people in the countryside, but it was shared in the cities, and some aspects of it were even practiced by the royal family. Local religion was based on the belief that the world was governed by supernatural powers and that these could be influenced by acts of devotion. Today this might be called superstition.

An Example of Local Religion   Villages frequently made vows to saints to have them intercede with God to prevent or end a natural disaster, such as hail, drought, or disease. Some chose certain saints because they were known as specialists, such as Saint Roch for disease or Saint Augustine for locusts. Others made their choices in response to signs, such as the repetition of hail on a particular saint's day. Still others held a lottery among a group of saints. The choice of a saint to whom to make a vow was usually made without the participation of the local clergy. Here is a description of how the town of Pareja, in the province of Guadalajara, chose two saints to protect it from the plague.

This town is devoted to the blessed saints Simon and Jude, apostles, and holds them as patrons and advocates. The old people were heard to say that this devotion was taken miraculously, because when there was a general plague in the town, they devoutly decided to celebrate the feast of the saint that our Lord should inspire them to choose, and hence they made twelve wax candles and put on each the name of an apostle, and lit them in front of the Holy Sacrament, proposing that the last candle that was live—for all of them had the same weight and wick—would be considered the devotion that they had to celebrate. . . . The last two candles that remained were those of Simon and Jude, and these saints were celebrated in perpetuity, and nowadays the feast is celebrated by giving and dividing up twelve cattle as charity to the inhabitants of the town and poor outsiders.

The Golden Age

While Spain faced continual warfare and uncertainty, in the realm of culture it experienced an era of unprecedented creativity and brilliance, known with good reason as the Golden Age.

The literature of the Golden Age is varied. In prose, poetry, and drama the period produced some of Spain's greatest writers and greatest creations.

Without doubt the greatest single literary product of the Golden Age, and one of the highlights of world literature, is Miguel de Cervantes's *Don Quixote*. Cervantes wrote his novel as a parody of the chivalric literature that was so popular in sixteenth-century Spain. Don Quixote, a minor nobleman driven mad by having read too many chivalric romances, sets out with his squire, the down-to-earth and plain-spoken Sancho Panza, to find the adventures he has read about in books. Such things do not occur in the real world, but Don Quixote refuses to see things as they really are, taking a peasant girl for a princess and windmills for giants. After numerous such "adventures" he is taken back to his village by people who have no sympathy for his imaginary world, and he dies.

One important literary innovation was the picaresque novel. In these novels the central characters are not the virtuous heroes of the chival-

Leading Writers of the Golden Age

Garcilaso de la Vega (1503–1536)
  Eclogues
Fernando de Rojas (1465?–1541?)
  La Celestina
Saint Teresa of Avila (1515–1582)
  Life, Letters
Saint John of the Cross (1542–1591)
  Spiritual Songs
Miguel de Cervantes Saavedra (1547–1616)
  Don Quixote, Exemplary Novels
Mateo Alemán (1547–1614?)
  Guzmán de Alfarache
Luís de Góngora y Argote (1561–1627)
  Solitudes
Lope de Vega (1562–1635)
  Fuenteovejuna
Francisco Gómez de Quevedo y Villegas (1580–1645)
  The Swindler, Dreams
Tirso de Molina (1584?–1648)
  The Joker of Seville
Pedro Calderón de la Barca (1600–1681)
  Life Is a Dream
Baltasar de Gracián (1601–1658)
  The Fault Finder

ric romances but rather transients and criminals who make their way through the world by their wits, deceiving and taking advantage of everyone they can.

The first picaresque novel was *Lazarillo de Tormes*, which was published anonymously in 1554. Lazarillo is the son of a miller who was executed for cheating his customers and a woman who worked as a servant. Still a boy, he sets off from Salamanca as the guide for a blind beggar. Since his master is very tightfisted and does not give him enough to eat, Lazarillo has to find ways of tricking him to get the food he wants. At one point he steals a sausage the blind man is going to eat and replaces it with a rotten turnip:

I swore blind I had nothing to do with it, but it was no use. I couldn't hide anything from that evil old man. He stood up, seized me by the head, and bent down to smell me. He must have got the scent like a bloodhound, for to satisfy himself . . . he grasped me firmly, forced my mouth wide open, and thrust his nose down my throat. His nose was long and sharp and his rage had made it a lot longer so its tip touched my gullet. What with that, my terror and the brief space of time which had not let the sausage settle and most of all the awful feeling of that enormous nose almost choking me, the deed and my greed were revealed and my master received his property back; for, before he could get his trunk out of my mouth my stomach was so upset that I brought it all up, and his nose and the half-digested sausage came out at the same time.

This period also produced a number of Spain's most important painters. Among them there were two truly outstanding figures. The first was Doménikos Theotokópoulos, El Greco (1541–1614), a Greek who came to Spain in the 1570's. His work was dominated by religious themes but stood out because of his brilliant colors and unusual distortion of human figures. The second was Diego Velázquez (1599–1660). Much of Velázquez's work portrays the royal family and aspects of court life. He was a master of composition, and a number of his greatest

Don Quixote

Tilting at Windmills

In a village of La Mancha the name of which I have no desire to re-
call, there lived not so long ago one of those gentlemen who always
have a lance in the rack, an ancient buckler, a skinny nag and a
greyhound for the chase. . . . This gentleman of ours was close on
to fifty, of a robust constitution but with little flesh on his bones
and a face that was lean and gaunt. . . . On those occasions when
he was at leisure, which was most of the year around, [he] was in
the habit of reading books of chivalry with such pleasure and devotion as to lead him almost wholly to forget the administration of his
estate. . . . In short, our gentleman became so immersed in his
reading that he spent whole nights from sundown to sunup and his
days from dawn to dusk in poring over his books, until, from so little sleeping and so much reading, his brain dried up and he went
completely out of his mind. . . .

   At this point they caught sight of thirty or forty windmills which
were standing on the plain there, and no sooner had Don Quixote
laid eyes upon them that he turned to his squire and said, "Fortune
is guiding our affairs better than we could have wished; for you see
there before you, friend Sancho Panza, some thirty or more lawless
giants with whom I mean to do battle. I shall deprive them of their
lives, and with the spoils from this encounter we shall begin to en-
rich ourselves; for this is righteous warfare, and it is a great service to God to remove so accursed a breed from the face of the
earth."

   "What giants?" asked Sancho Panza.

   "Those that you see there," replied his master, "those with the
long arms, some of which are as much as two leagues in length."

"But look, your Grace, those are not giants but windmills, and what appear to be arms are their wings which, when whirled in the breeze, cause the millstone to go."

"It is plain to be seen," said Don Quixote, "that you have had little experience in this matter of adventures. If you are afraid, go off to one side and say your prayers while I am engaging them in fierce unequal combat."

Saying this, he gave spurs to his steed Rocinante, without paying heed to Sancho's warning that these were truly windmills and not giants that he was riding forth to attack. Nor even when he was close upon them did he perceive what they really were, but shouted at the top of his lungs, "Do not seek to flee, cowards and vile creatures that you are, for it is but a single knight with whom you have to deal!"

At that moment a little wind came up and the big wings began turning.

"Though you flourish as many arms as did the giant Briareus," said Don Quixote when he perceived this, "you still shall have to answer to me. . . ." He bore down upon them at a full gallop and fell upon the first mill that stood in his way, giving a thrust at the wing, which was whirling at such a speed his lance was broken into bits and both horse and horeseman went rolling over the plain, very much battered indeed. Sancho upon his donkey came hurrying to his master's assistance as fast as he could, but when he reached the spot, the knight was unable to move, so great was the shock with which he and Rocinante had hit the ground.

"God help us!" exclaimed Sancho, "did I not tell your Grace to look well, that those were nothing but windmills, a fact which no one could fail to see unless he had other mills of the same sort in his head?"

How the kitchen of a village house might have looked at the time of Don Quixote. This house in El Toboso, province of Toledo, is called the House of Dulcinea. Courtesy of the Tourist Office of Spain

works, such as *The Maids of Honor* and *The Surrender of Breda,* allow the viewer to look in on a scene, almost becoming part of it.

The Last Habsburg

The last Habsburg King of Spain was Charles II (ruled 1665–1700). He bore only the faintest resemblance to his great predecessors, Charles I and Philip II, but he was a fitting physical testament to the Habsburg practice of marrying within the family. Charles was mentally retarded and suffered from a number of physical and psychological illnesses that kept him in bed for most of his life. In his last years he also suffered from fits, which led people to believe that he was bewitched and to call on exorcists to relieve him.

Charles was married twice but he had no children, so he had to decide on his successor. Initially there were three candidates, but the one with the strongest claim, the grandson of Philip IV's daughter, died in 1699. That left a French candidate, Philip of Anjou, and an Austrian candidate, the Archduke Charles. Charles II decided on Philip of Anjou and stuck to his choice in the face of tremendous pressure, including that of his German wife.

The Frenchman became Philip V when Charles died on November 1, 1700, but he was challenged two years later when Austria, England, and Holland declared war. This War of the Spanish Succession ended in 1714 when Philip renounced any interest in the French throne. Spain lost its possessions in Italy and the Low Countries to the Austrian Habsburgs and Gibraltar to England, but this was less significant than the changes the war brought about in Spain itself.

The Eighteenth Century

The War of the Spanish Succession brought out the divisions between Castile and Aragon once again. In 1705 Catalonia backed the Austrian claimant. Aragon and Valencia did the same a little later. In so doing they picked the losing side and this time losing bore a heavy price. The House of Bourbon, represented by Philip V, had none of the respect, however grudging, for traditional local institutions that its Habsburg predecessors had had, and the king promptly abolished them. A new system of government was announced in 1716, changing Spain from a set of autonomous realms united only in the person of the monarch into a single, unified, and increasingly centralized state. From Ferdinand and Isabella to Charles II Spanish rulers had been kings—or queen—of Castile and kings of Aragon; now they were kings of Spain.

The Bourbon kings were not content with these administrative

The Bourbon Kings of Spain, 1700–1808

Philip V	1700–1724, 1724–1746
Luís I	1724
Ferdinand VI	1746–1759
Charles III	1759–1788
Charles IV	1788–1808

changes. They also sought to revive the economy and rebuild Spanish power. For Spain, the eighteenth century was a period of reform and recovery.

The Enlightenment

The experience of reform was something Spain shared with most other European states in the eighteenth century. This approach to reform is known as enlightened despotism. Often associated with specific monarchs like Catherine the Great in Russia, Frederick the Great in Prussia, Joseph II in Austria, and Charles III in Spain, it was also connected with an intellectual movement called the Enlightenment.

What was the Enlightenment? It was the spread of an intellectual revolution, of new ways of looking at the world and at human society. This revolution was based on a number of great scientific and philosophical breakthroughs that took place in the seventeenth century. Thinkers such as Sir Isaac Newton (1642–1727), Sir Francis Bacon (1561–1626), René Descartes (1596–1650), Thomas Hobbes (1588–1679), and John Locke (1632–1704) created new views of the universe and proposed new ways of thinking about natural and human matters. Their work challenged traditional beliefs and the authority of the

FRANCE

ANDORRA

Mediterranean Sea

BALEARIC ISLANDS

HISTORICAL REGIONS
c. 1750

Boundary lines of
modern-day provinces

CATALONIA

• Barcelona

ARAGON

NAVARRE

BASQUE COUNTRY

Valencia
• VALENCIA

MURCIA

Burgos
•
OLD CASTILE

Madrid
•
Toledo
•
NEW CASTILE

ANDALUSIA

Granada
•

Oviedo
•
ASTURIAS

LEÓN

Salamanca
•

EXTREMADURA

Seville
•

Strait of Gibraltar

GALICIA

PORTUGAL

Atlantic Ocean

Catholic Church in which those beliefs were based.

In the eighteenth century the great innovations were spread by a number of French writers known as the *philosophes*. Men such as François-Marie Arouet Voltaire (1694–1778) and Denis Diderot (1713–1784) were not original thinkers but brilliant publicists who brought a sense of intellectual independence and skepticism of established authority to a broad audience. The greatest monument of the Enlightenment was the *Encyclopedia*, 38 volumes, compiled under the direction of Diderot, that claimed to bring together all human knowledge. (See *The Land and People of France*.)

The basic message of the *philosophes* was that the world could be known through careful observation and that the institutions of society could, and should, be changed in order to reach the goal of humankind, which was, simply, happiness. If misery existed in the world, it was not because men and women were naturally evil, but because of institutions that were tradition bound or irrational. If these were changed, then misery would be eliminated.

Chocolate and Fried Salt Pork

Spain too had its Enlightenment, and it began in a most unexpected place, far from the usual centers of Spanish intellectual life. Benito Jerónimo Feijóo (1676–1764) was the son of a minor noble from Galicia. He became a Benedictine monk and professor of theology at the University of Oviedo. Beginning in 1726 he published two collections of essays, *Universal Critical Theater* and *Erudite Letters*. These fourteen volumes took a critical approach to established beliefs in a wide range of fields: medicine, politics, education, history, science, and philosophy, among others. They also introduced the major work of contemporary foreign thinkers to Spanish readers. Feijóo's work found a large and enthusiastic audience; by 1786 it had gone through fifteen editions and was more popular than any other Spanish book except *Don Quixote*.

The real meaning of the Enlightenment is most apparent in ordinary matters of everyday life. Nothing was too small or insignificant to be questioned or to be tested by scientific methods. In Volume Five of his *Universal Critical Theater* Feijóo explains how he used the scientific method to disprove a popular belief about eating habits.

When I was a boy, everyone said that it was very dangerous to eat anything right after the [morning] hot chocolate. My mind, for some reason which I could not then perhaps have explained very well, was so skeptical of this common comprehension that I decided to make the experiment. . . . Immediately after my chocolate, I ate a large quantity of fried salt pork, and I felt fine that day and for a long time thereafter, wherefore I had the satisfaction of laughing at those who were possessed by this fear.

The new ideas spread through other channels as well. Magazines such as *The Thinker* and *The Spirit of the Best Newspapers Published in Europe* provided criticism of Spanish institutions and kept interested Spaniards in touch with developments in other countries. After 1760 people in most of the major cities created Sociedades Ecónomicas de Amigos del País (Economic Societies of Friends of the Country). These were cultural centers dedicated to spreading the latest ideas, especially about economic questions.

It is important not to exaggerate the spread of the Enlightenment in Spain. Neither the Economic Societies nor the newspapers and magazines reached a mass audience. The most widely read of the journals had a circulation of only 765 copies, while the members of the Economic Societies numbered only a few thousand. In both cases, the enlightened came from the social elite of nobles, clerics, doctors, lawyers, and government officials. They were a tiny percentage of the population; the vast majority of Spaniards were untouched by the Enlightenment.

The Enlightenment in Spain also differed in some respects from that in other countries, especially France. Enlightened Spaniards were less likely to be concerned with abstract philosophical questions than with the more practical question of how to improve the social and economic organization of their country. And while they criticized specific practices of the Catholic Church, they were much less likely to go further and criticize Catholic beliefs.

"It Is Not Enough That the People Be Quiet; It Is Necessary That They Be Happy"

Some of the ideas of the Enlightenment were taken up by royal officials who sought to use them to achieve their own, more specific concerns: to make their countries function more effectively and efficiently in order to increase their wealth and power. Enlightened reform was a kind of eighteenth-century *perestroika*, or restructuring, designed to strengthen the state and the economy without changing the political system as a whole.

Gaspar Melchor de Jovellanos (1744–1811) was one of the leading figures of the Spanish Enlightenment. He was an intellectual with wide-ranging interests, who wrote poetry, plays, treatises on education, travel accounts, and works of history. He was also a practical thinker, concerned with reforming numerous aspects of Spanish life. As a government official he tried to realize some of those reforms.

The purpose of reform for Jovellanos was to allow the nation to prosper and the individual to achieve happiness. The role of government was to create the conditions in which both were possible by balancing

Portrait of enlightened reformer Gaspar Melchor de Jovellanos, by Francisco de Goya.
Museo del Prado, Madrid

government vigilance and individual freedom. The new laws were not limited to what we might consider the most important aspects of national life, such as the economy, but even dealt with individuals' use of their leisure time. Even leisure had economic and political implications. This was the subject of the *Study of Spectacles and Public Entertainments in Spain,* which Jovellanos wrote in 1790 at the request of the Council of Castile, which was considering changing the relevant laws.

Working people need entertainments but not spectacles. It is not necessary for the government to entertain them; it only need allow them to entertain themselves. In the few days, in the brief hours, they can devote to recreation they will seek and invent their entertainments; it is enough to give them freedom and protection to enjoy them. . . .

But why is it that in most Spanish villages the people do not have any entertainments?. . . One of the most frequent causes is the zeal of too many magistrates, who are convinced that the perfection of local government requires the subjugation of the people. . . . This idea has reached even the most miserable hamlets, so that the unhappy laborer, who has sweated over the land and slept in the fields all week, cannot shout in the village square on Saturday night or sing a song to his girlfriend.

It is not enough that the people be quiet; it is necessary that they be happy and only unfeeling hearts or heads lacking any sense of humanity, or even of good politics, could think of achieving the one without the other.

A free and happy people will be active and hard working and as a result will be well behaved and obey the laws. The more it enjoys the more it will love its government and obey it. The more it enjoys the more it will fear disorder and respect the authority charged with repressing it. It will have more interest in enriching itself because it knows that its pleasure will increase with its wealth. To put it bluntly: It will seek its happiness more ardently because it will be certain of enjoying it. . . .

The magistrate's vigilance should be like that of the Supreme Being: certain and constant but invisible; known to all but apparent to no one; close to disorder so as to suppress it and to liberty so as to protect it. The good magistrate should protect the people in its pastimes . . . and let them devote themselves freely to them. If he must be present himself it should be as a father who takes pleasure in the joy of his children, not as a tyrant envious of the happiness of his slaves.

Three Reforms

Eighteenth-century reform was wide-ranging but it centered on three areas. One concern was to overcome the fragmentation of power and

An English Visitor Describes the Workhouse at Cádiz, 1786

Joseph Townsend was a doctor and Anglican priest. He was the author of a number of books on subjects as varied as religion, medicine, geology, political philosophy, and economics. He traveled through Spain in 1786 and 1787 and, as was common at the time, later published an account of his trip. Townsend was prepared to praise Spanish superiority where he saw it, but he was also highly critical of many things, especially in Spain's economy. For example, he was unfavorably impressed by the scale of charity offered by the church; in the city of Córdoba he claimed that every day the bishop provided bread for over one thousand people. In Cádiz, in contrast, he praised a more "rational" approach to dealing with the poor.

This building is large and lofty, handsome and commodious. In it are received the poor of every nation, who are unable to maintain them-

authority and strengthen the power of the Crown. This was one of the first things the Bourbons did in Spain, subjecting the entire country to the same laws and then, in 1749, establishing royal agents, known as intendants, throughout the country.

A second, related concern was to reduce the power and independence of the Catholic Church. In 1761 Charles III prohibited the publication of Papal declarations in Spain without royal permission. The Jesuit order, with its special vow of obedience to the Pope, was a major target, and in 1766 the Jesuits were expelled from the country. The

selves, and in the first place, orphans, deserted children and the aged, who are past the capability for labour, the blind, the lame, idiots and mad people. . . .

Neatness universally prevails, and all who are here received are clean, well clothed and have plenty of the best provisions. Care is taken to instruct them in Christian doctrines and every six months the young people are publicly examined. Their education is to read, to write, to cast accounts. . . . The boys are trained to weaving and to various crafts; the girls spin wool, flax and cotton; they knit, make lace or are employed in plain work. . . .

To encourage industry an account is kept for each individual, wherein he is made debtor to the house at the rate of about seven pence a day and has credit given him for all the work he does; and should the balance be, as often happens, in his favour, it is paid to him whenever he can make it appear to the satisfaction of the directors that he is able to establish himself without their future aid. . . .

Inquisition remained in place, but Charles III appointed a more progressive Inquisitor General and required that all cases against royal officials be submitted to him. Reformers also wanted to replace traditional forms of charity, in which vast amounts of food or money were distributed to beggars. This was now seen as an encouragement to idleness; society would be better off if beggars were put into *hospicios*, workhouses, where they were put to some useful task and earned their keep.

The third, and most pressing, concern was to strengthen the economy. The government established its own factories, for tapestries in Madrid and woolens in Guadalajara, and imported foreign craftsmen to teach the latest skills to Spaniards. These initiatives were financial disasters. The Bourbons also sought to encourage manufacturing by removing the stigma attached to manual labor. In 1773 nobles were permitted to work at crafts without losing their status, and ten years later members of a number of trades, such as tailors, shoemakers, and carpenters, were allowed to hold office in local government.

Reformers had much more interest in the land and agriculture, which they saw as the foundation of the country's prosperity. Their goal was to increase agricultural production, especially that of grain, by encouraging the individual farmer. In Andalusia and Estremadura, where there were large numbers of landless laborers, municipal governments were ordered to distribute uncultivated land. In 1765 German settlers were brought in to start colonies in unpopulated areas of the south.

Reformers also attacked the Mesta, the organization of owners of migrant sheep. Since the Reconquest of southern Spain the Mesta had enjoyed a number of privileges, such as the right to run their sheep across cultivated land during the semiannual migration. This right was abolished in 1786, and two years later farmers were allowed to put fences around their land.

The Empire

If Spain was to revive its economy, it would have to make better use of its empire. England stood as a clear example of how an empire could contribute to national power, and Spanish reformers sought to make their own colonies more profitable. This meant increasing revenues to the Crown and increasing trade between Spain and the colonies.

Early in the century the Crown created a number of companies that were given monopolies on trade with specific regions. More important was the gradual dismantling of the monopoly on colonial trade enjoyed by Seville and the movement toward freer trade between Spain and the colonies. In 1765 nine Spanish ports, including Barcelona, were allowed to trade with America, and by 1789 there was almost completely free trade within the empire.

These policies were highly successful. Between 1778 and 1790 Spanish colonial trade quadrupled. The strengthening of the economic ties between Spain and its American colonies was accompanied by more effective political control. In the seventeenth century, the creoles, the native-born whites, had filled many government offices in Spanish America and had come to enjoy positions of influence and prestige. But the creoles were more independent of the Crown than the Bourbon kings were prepared to accept, and in the eighteenth century they were replaced by officials sent from Spain. This led to dissatisfaction among the creole elite, which would culminate in 1808 with the revolts for independence.

Goya

The eighteenth century was not a period of brilliant cultural achievement in Spain. Even so, it did produce one of the country's greatest artists, Francisco de Goya (1746–1828). Goya stands out even in the development of European art as a whole. He is the first truly modern artist, the first artist to confront the reality of a rapidly changing and confusing world and to describe it from the point of view of ordinary men and women.

Goya was a man of the Enlightenment, so religion was never very important in his work, but his world was not governed by reason either. The French Revolution of 1789 had unleashed powerful new forces across Europe. These were not under anyone's control, nor were they fully understood; the hopes raised by that revolution were largely frustrated. Goya's paintings and drawings from this period, and especially from the years after 1808, when French armies brought the revolution

For some years back they have received from Madrid even the most
trifling appointments in the administration. . . . The result has been
a jealousy and perpetual hatred between the [Spaniards] and the creoles. The most miserable European, without education and without
intellectual cultivation, thinks himself superior to the whites born in
the new continent. He knows that . . . he may one day reach places to
which the access is almost interdicted to the natives, even to those
distinguished for their talents, knowledge and moral qualities. The
natives prefer the denomination of Americans to that of creoles. . . .
We frequently hear proudly declared "I am not a Spaniard, I am an
American!"—words which betray the workings of a long resentment.
. . . The abuse of the laws, the false measures of the colonial government, the example of the United States of America, and the influence
of the opinions of the age, have relaxed the ties which formerly
united more closely the Spanish creoles to the European Spaniards.

to Spain, are full of powerful images that reflect this disappointment,
as well as the anxiety and fear that accompanied it.

The major events of Goya's career are well known, but much of the
rest of his life—his personality and his opinions—is obscure. He was
born in the Aragonese village of Fuendetodos. His family was not well
off, but they could give him some education and art training. He was
able to travel and study in Italy in 1770 and 1771. In 1775 he received
his first commission from Madrid, to do some illustrations for the
Royal Tapestry Factory. After that success came rapidly. Goya knew
how to work within the system to advance his career. By 1786 he had
been appointed court painter, and when Charles IV came to the throne
he was named painter to the King. Goya suffered a major illness in

The Colossus *by Goya: the forces of war and revolution unleashed?* Museo del Prado, Madrid

1792–1793; he nearly died and was left permanently deaf. From that point on all in his work is touched by a sense of sadness and pessimism, which reached its peak during the War of Independence against the French (1808–1814). In 1824 he left Spain for France. Four years later he died in Bordeaux.

Goya's working life covered over half a century and a number of different artistic forms. Much of his work was done on commission—for example, religious paintings and portraits, as well as the tapestry illustrations. In all of these he was a subversive. This is clearest in his *Family of Charles IV*, painted in 1798. When the French writer Théophile Gautier saw it in the middle of the nineteenth century, he said that it looked like a picture of "the corner baker and his wife after they had won the lottery." Goya dared paint this unimpressive looking bunch as they were and did not bother to ennoble their appearance, which was the usual practice in such portraits.

Goya's greatest achievements came in those works he did for himself and in which he was under no constraints. The first of these was a series of etchings known as the *Caprices*. He began them with the Enlightenment aim of pointing out the stupidities of society in order to eliminate them. By the end he had lost his faith in progress and the triumph of reason. Through the ambiguities of lighting and setting he created a sense of irrationality, a world in which everyday scenes became frightening.

The horrors of the War of Independence led to his paintings *The Second of May, 1808* and *The Third of May, 1808*, as well as to another set of etchings, *The Disasters of War*. The etchings were Goya's private response to the conflict. They were not intended for the public and were not printed until 1862. *The Disasters of War* are the forerunners of photojournalism. They present an observed reality at its cruelest. Goya made no attempt to hide anything; the violence comes from both sides.

The Art of Modern War

In the nineteenth and twentieth centuries Spaniards were the first to experience the most modern forms of warfare. Guerrilla warfare was invented during the War of Independence, 1808–1814. The word itself is Spanish, meaning "little war." The saturation bombing of civilian targets from airplanes was first used in the Spanish Civil War, 1936–1939.

Perhaps for this reason it has been Spanish artists who have captured the brutality and horror of modern war most strongly. In his two paintings of the popular uprising against the French on May 2, 1808, and the French reprisals the next day, Francisco de Goya shows the viciousness of the popular revolt and the terror of the invaders' response. In Goya's painting the members of the firing squad are faceless, anonymous; in Pablo Picasso's painting of the bombing of Guernica in April 1937 the enemy is far above and totally invisible.

In both artists' work, the central figures are ordinary men and women. The emotions they display are those of ordinary people threatened with violent death: fear and terror. There is little bravery; there are no heroes.

The Third of May, 1808 *by Goya.*   Museo del Prado, Madrid

These paintings differ radically from an earlier view of war. Diego Velázquez's painting of the Dutch surrender of Breda to the Spanish in 1625 shows war as a glorious and civilized exchange between gentlemen. There is no blood or suffering anywhere to be seen.

Guernica *by Pablo Picasso.*   Museo del Prado, Madrid

The Surrender of Breda *by Diego de Velázquez.*   Museo del Prado, Madrid

The Family of Charles IV *by Goya.*   Museo del Prado, Madrid

Although he undoubtedly sympathized with his compatriots in their struggle against the invader, he makes no apologies for their actions. Patriotism, he tells us, is not an excuse for inhumanity.

Goya's pessimism culminated in the *Black Paintings*, a set of frescoes he painted on the walls of his house between 1820 and 1823. These too were private works. They depict monstrous beings in a world without any logic or reason, a world of violence and evil without any cause or explanation, a world ruled by chaos.

No other artist of that time speaks to us today as does Goya. We do not need to know history or mythology to feel the impact of his images. Even those works that describe specific historical events of his day tell us something about the events of our own.

The Making of Liberal Spain, 1808–1898

In Spain, as in the rest of Europe, the most important developments during the nineteenth and early twentieth centuries were industrialization and the installation of constitutional, political systems. Manufacturing—but a manufacturing changed in nature—became a more important part of the economy. Independent small-scale producers working with simple hand tools gave way to larger workshops and factories where people who owned nothing but their labor worked for others on steam—and later electrically—powered machines in return for a wage. In politics, the absolute monarchy that had ruled Spain since the sixteenth century was replaced by a system in which the government was chosen in elections by the people—or rather, by those individuals who were deemed worthy of having a political voice. Both these developments created tensions and conflicts that were not fully resolved. Spain's humiliating defeat at the hands of the United States in 1898 triggered a national crisis of conscience and stimulated the emergence of movements to challenge the country's political institutions.

The Creation of Freedom

Late in 1807 the armies of the French emperor Napoleon invaded Spain. This triggered the crisis that would lead to the establishment of a constitutional system.

On March 16, 1808, popular protest in the city of Aranjuez led King Charles IV (ruled 1788–1808) to abdicate in favor of his son, Ferdinand VII (ruled 1808–1833). In May Napoleon called both to Bayonne, where he forced them to renounce the throne in favor of his brother Joseph Bonaparte, who became King José I (1808–1814).

This interference in Spain's affairs prompted a widespread popular revolt. The uprising began in Madrid on May 2 and quickly turned into the guerrilla war whose brutality was captured by the great artist Francisco de Goya. The term "guerrilla war," which is so familiar to us today as meaning a struggle for some political or social goal carried out by armed citizens outside the regular army, was created in Spain at this time. This War of Independence lasted until 1814 and posed such a continual problem for Napoleon that it was known as the "Spanish ulcer." In the end a combined Spanish and British force commanded by the Duke of Wellington was able to throw the French out of Spain.

While the war raged, Spain experimented with new political forms. A Regency Council, which governed unoccupied Spain in the absence of Ferdinand VII, summoned a Cortes that met in Cadíz from September 1810 to September 1813. Led by a small but brilliant group of liberals such as Agustín Argüelles (1765–1844), the Count of Toreno (1766–1844), and Diego Muñoz Torrero (1761–1829), the Cortes drafted a new constitution, which was proclaimed on March 19, 1812.

The constitution brought liberalism to Spain. It declared that political power lay with the people represented in a Cortes elected by all males twenty-five or older, and that this Cortes would make the laws. Ministers were appointed by the king but were responsible to the legislature, and the king's veto power was very limited.

This was a revolutionary reordering of political power, but the liberal revolution was much more sweeping than this. It also totally changed the framework of Spanish society. The privileges of the aristocracy, the

The Limits of Liberalism

Liberalism was based on the belief that political sovereignty lay in the people, not in a monarch, that governments should be chosen by the people, and that all people were equal before the law. But who were the people? Who could vote? Who had equal rights?

Not all Spanish liberals gave exactly the same answers to these questions. In Spain, as across Europe, when liberals spoke about the people, they did not mean everybody. Liberalism's definition of the people was limited, although it did expand over time.

The first and most durable limitation on equality was that it applied to men only. Spanish women did not have the right to vote until 1933. Women, and especially married women, also had fewer legal rights than men. When a woman got married, she became a legal appendage of her husband. The Civil Code told wives that they should obey their

clergy, the regions, the guilds, and other groups were abolished in the name of liberty and equality. The power of the nobility and of ecclesiastical courts such as the Inquisition also disappeared as the state assumed direct jurisdiction over all its territory and all its citizens.

The Constitution of Cádiz became the symbol of Spanish liberalism. It also became a model for liberals across Europe and was even adopted, briefly, in Italy and Portugal. But the constitution was short-lived; Ferdinand VII revoked it when he was restored to the throne in 1814.

Ferdinand, backed by the church, some of the nobility, and some of the peasantry, rejected liberalism in favor of a return to absolute rule.

husbands and prescribed jail terms of 5 to 15 days for disobedience. A wife had to live where her husband did and could not even take a trip without his permission. Only with the death of her husband could a woman recover her legal rights.

But not even all men were equal in liberal societies. Liberals believed that only men who owned property had the independence necessary to make informed judgments on public affairs, so virtually all liberal constitutions had property requirements for voting. (Some also had literacy requirements.) These requirements were very restrictive. Under the Constitution of 1837, which was written by the progressives, only 2 percent of the population could vote. The moderates' Constitution of 1845 cut that to less than 1 percent. The Constitution of 1876 initially imposed property requirements, but universal male suffrage was finally introduced in 1890.

The liberals enjoyed support in the army, the nobility, the middle classes, and the urban lower classes. The liberals eventually won, but only after a long and fierce struggle that included a number of military revolts and a civil war, the Carlist War, which lasted from 1833 to 1840.

After 1840 constitutional government was firmly established in Spain, but the country's political situation remained troubled. The liberals were divided into two large groups known as Moderates and Progressives. Although they shared many basic ideas, they disagreed over how many people should be allowed to vote and whether local governments should be elected or appointed. Queen Isabella II (1833–1868) sympathized with the Moderates and did not want to give the Progressives a turn in government. The Progressives responded by relying on sympathetic army officers to bring them to power through military coups.

Restoration

Isabella II was finally chased from the throne by a revolution in 1868, but after six years of instability a military coup brought her son, Alfonso XII (ruled 1874–1885), to the throne. These events opened what is known as the Restoration, the period of greatest political stability since 1808. The new political system was the handiwork of Antonio Cánovas del Castillo (1828–1897). Cánovas was a great admirer of the British parliamentary system, and especially of the peaceful alternation in power of the two principal parties, which he saw as its most important feature.

Cánovas was so determined to create a copy of that system of stability for Spain that he was prepared to base it on systematic electoral corruption rather than run the risk of elections producing an undesired result. On the one hand, the two main political parties agreed to alternate more or less regularly in power. On the other hand, local men of influence, called *caciques* (from an Amerindian word for chief), delivered the votes of their followers to the candidate the government wanted to win. When this was not sufficient, the government used force or other forms of fraud, such as locating voting booths in a pigpen or hiring gangs to cast votes in the names of dead people whose names still appeared on the voting lists.

Everything worked quite smoothly so long as there were no organized political parties beyond the Liberals and Conservatives, on which the system was based. When such parties did appear at the end of the nineteenth century, the system became increasingly unworkable and eventually gave way to a military dictatorship.

Literature

For most of the nineteenth century Spanish literature was influenced by foreign models. In the 1820's and 1830's the most important literary current was romanticism. Influenced by Sir Walter Scott, Victor Hugo, and Lord Byron, among others, the romantic writers were poets and dramatists whose works emphasized individual liberty and the importance of love. They often turned to the historical past for the inspiration for their work.

Romanticism also encouraged writers to describe local customs, especially those that might be considered most typical. In Spain this type of writing was known as *costumbrismo*. It usually took the form of brief accounts of some aspect of local color. The best of the *costumbrista* writers was Mariano José de Larra (1809–1837), whose articles had a sharp, satirical edge. His most famous sketch, "Come Back Tomorrow," in which a visitor cannot get served by a government official, was a critique of Spanish laziness but also captured the frustration of all people who have had to deal with government bureaucracy.

Padilla's painting of Juana the Mad with the corpse of her husband is a good example of how Romantic artists drew inspiration from historical themes. Museo del Prado, Madrid

Romanticism, with its interest in the historical past, contributed to reviving regional languages and literatures across Europe. In Spain it helped revive Catalan literature, which had languished since the end of the fifteenth century. Beginning in 1833, when Carlos Aribau published his "Ode to the Fatherland," Catalan literature experienced what is known as the Renaissance, or *Renaixença*. Aribau's poem begins:

> *Farewell, hills, farewell forever,*
> *O uneven mountains which, there in my fatherland,*
> *From the clouds and the sky distinguish you from afar,*
> *Through eternal rest, through the color most blue.*

Perhaps the most famous Catalan literary figure of the nineteenth century was Jacinto Verdaguer (1845–1902), a priest who wrote both epic poems and religious lyric verse.

Later in the century the novel emerged as the dominant literary form in Spain. The new importance of this genre was due to Benito Pérez Galdós (1843–1920), a disciple of the great realistic novelists Charles Dickens and Honoré de Balzac. Pérez Galdós was a prolific writer; he produced the *National Episodes*, a series of forty-six novels narrating the history of Spain in the nineteenth century, as well as thirty-four other novels, twenty-four plays, and fifteen volumes of other writings.

Leading Figures of Spanish Romanticism

Theater

Angel de Saavedra, Duque de Rivas (1791–1865)
Don Alvaro: or, The Force of Destiny
Juan Eugenio Hartzenbusch (1806–1880)
The Lovers of Teruel
José Zorilla (1817–1893)
Don Juan Tenorio

Poetry

José de Espronceda (1808–1842)
The Student of Salamanca, The Devil World
Gustavo Adolfo Bécquer (1836–1870)
Rhymes, Legends

The great masterpiece of nineteenth-century fiction did not come from Galdós but from Leopoldo Alas, under the pen name of Clarín (1852–1901). His novel *The Judge's Wife* criticizes the corrupt bourgeois society of a provincial capital, Oviedo. The central character, Ana, the young wife of an elderly judge, is attracted to two other men, one of whom is her confessor.

The best female writer of nineteenth-century Spain was also a novelist. Emilia Pardo Bazán (1852–1921) was born in La Coruña, Galicia, and her greatest novel, *The House of Ulloa*, is a scathing critique of the Galician nobility and the brutality of rural life in her native region. Pardo Bazán was also a feminist. In 1916 she became the first female professor at the University of Madrid, although the Minister of Education had to appoint her over the objections of the university.

The authors mentioned so far are all still widely read in Spain today. The only nineteenth-century Spanish writer to receive the highest form of international recognition is now almost forgotten in Spain. José Echegaray (1832–1916) was awarded the Nobel Prize for Literature in 1904. Echegaray combined successful careers as an engineer, university professor, and politician with writing plays. These lack any serious theme or character development and turn solely on thoroughly improbable situations; Echegaray would probably have been a success writing for television.

The Generation of 1898 and the Question of Spain

Right at the end of the century Spain produced a literary movement of its own. The Generation of 1898, as this group of writers is called, wrote in response to Spain's greatest national humiliation, its defeat in the Spanish-American War of 1898.

A Spanish regiment in Cuba, 1898.   Biblioteca Nacional, Madrid

Spain lost the bulk of its American empire in the first two decades of the nineteenth century. After 1821 only Cuba and Puerto Rico were left, but after 1860 Cubans were increasingly unhappy with Spanish rule. An independence revolt broke out in 1868, and it took the Spanish authorities ten years to suppress it. A second revolt, inspired by José Martí (1853–1895), started in 1895. Cuba had come increasingly into the economic orbit of the United States, and influential Americans, especially the newspaper magnate William Randolph Hearst (1863–1951), began to demand that the United States intervene against Spain. The pressure on President William McKinley increased after the American battleship *Maine* was sunk in Havana's harbor on February 15, 1898. The United States declared war on Spain on April 20, 1898.

Spain was badly defeated. Even worse, it was totally humiliated. Admiral Dewey destroyed the Pacific fleet at Manila on May 1; Spain's Caribbean fleet was defeated in Santiago de Cuba harbor on July 3 at the cost of one American life. The war ended on August 12, and in

December Spain signed the Treaty of Paris, under which it left Cuba and transferred Puerto Rico, the Philippines, and Guam to the United States.

The disaster of 1898 led Spanish intellectuals to think about the overall health of their nation and to consider ways of countering what they saw as its decline to second-rate status. The analyses made by the members of the Generation of 1898 did not consider Spain's social and economic problems, but addressed the much more intangible question of the nature and state of the national soul. Given this orientation, it is

Members of the Generation of 1898

Azorín (José Martínez Ruiz) (1873–1967)
  The Route of Don Quixote
Pío Baroja (1879–1956)
  Way of Perfection
Ángel Ganivet (1865–1898)
  Spain: An Interpretation
Antonio Machado (1875–1939)
  Fields of Castile
Ramiro de Maéztu (1874–1936)
  Defense of Spanishness
Miguel de Unamuno (1864–1936)
  Concerning Traditionalism
Ramón del Valle Inclán (1866?–1936)
  Iberian Circuit

not surprising that their concern for their country's future did not lead them to become active in politics, although Miguel de Unamuno did flirt briefly with socialism and Ramiro de Maéztu became an advocate of military dictatorship.

These writers can be placed in two basic categories: those who felt that Spain had to return to its traditions and those who felt that it had to become more "European."

The first of these approaches can be seen in Ángel Ganivet's *Spain: An Interpretation*, which appeared in 1897, before the Spanish-American War. For Ganivet, Spain had to recover its guiding ideas, what he called *ideas madres*, and overcome the *abulia*, or paralysis of will, from which it suffered. Ganivet never defined these ideas, but his concern was with spiritual rather than economic development. Spain had to recover its real traditions rather than look to Europe for guidance.

Unamuno shared with Ganivet a belief in a national character, which he called *casticismo* (purity or tradition) and which was found in the country's ruling elite and was responsible for Spain's decline. Fortunately, a vital eternal tradition, or *infrahistoria*, thrived among the common people and was the soil that would allow the seeds of European ideas to flourish and revitalize the country. Unamuno did not deal at length with economic questions, but he at least realized that they were important.

Economic Change

Throughout the nineteenth century more Spaniards worked on the land than in any other economic activity, and the crops they produced were the basis of the economy. Wheat was the most important crop, especially in Castile; but when inexpensive grain from North America be-

The Regeneration of Spain

Ángel Ganivet, *Spain: An Interpretation*:

Just as I believe that for enterprises of material conquest many
European countries are superior to us, so do I believe that for the
creation of ideas there is none with finer aptitude than ourselves.
Our spirit seems rude, because it has been coarsened by brutal
strife; it seems flabby because it has been nourished on ridiculous
notions, copied without discernment from outside; and it seems uno-
riginal, because it has lost the bold faith in its own ideas, and looks
outside for what it has within. We must make a collective act of con-
trition, we must return to our natural form. . . . In this way, we shall
have spiritual food for ourselves and for our family, now wandering

gan to arrive on the European market in the 1870's, Spanish wheat
farmers found themselves in trouble.

Spanish farmers were able to respond to new opportunities when
they arose. Foreign demand for wines, olive oil, and citrus fruits led
Spanish farmers greatly to increase the amount of land they devoted to
these crops and made them some of Spain's most important exports.

Spain began to industrialize quite early, and the economy continued
to grow and change throughout the nineteenth century. But the rate of
economic growth in Spain was less than in many other European countries, so even though the nation was moving ahead, in relative terms it
found itself falling further behind.

Cotton textiles, which everywhere were the first products to be produced in factories and on steam-powered machinery, got underway in

about the world begging for it; and our material conquests may yet
be fruitful, because after our rebirth we shall have myriads of our
own race on whom to impress the seal of our spirit.

Miguel de Unamuno, *Concerning Traditionalism*:

. . . The mental misery of Spain began with the isolation forced on us
by a policy . . . which prevented the entry of the European
Reformation. . . . Only by opening our windows to the breezes from
Europe, soaking ourselves in the atmosphere of the continent, having faith that we will not lose ourselves if we do it, Europeanizing
ourselves in order to make Spain and plunging ourselves in the people, will we regenerate this moral steppe. I regenerate my blood with
air from outside, not by breathing in what I exhale.

Catalonia in the eighteenth century. Spain's political upheavals in the
first thirty years of the nineteenth century blocked development, but
new machines were introduced rapidly after 1830. Work in the textile
mills of Catalonia was described in 1911 by Ralph Odell, an agent for
the United States Department of Commerce:

There are three characteristics of the cotton industry that impress an
American upon entering a Spanish cotton mill: First, the large number of
operatives required; second, the predominance of female employees (only
about 15 percent are males); third, the wide range of fabrics produced in
each factory.

Wages paid in Spanish cotton mills are considerably lower than those pre-
vailing in the United States, ranging from $1.43 per week to $5.02 paid to

Working Children

Children had always started work very young, but before industrialization they usually worked within a family setting, on a farm or in a small workshop. Even when they went out to apprentice to a stranger, that person was expected to act as a father as well as an employer. In the industrial world children worked for strangers who had no interest in them beyond the amount of work they could do and no responsibility toward them beyond paying their wages.

Children were introduced to the "real world" very quickly and it was often neither easy nor pleasant. Dolores Ibarruri ("La Pasionaria") (1895–1989), who later became a leader of the Spanish Communist Party, was born and grew up in the mining districts of Bilbao. The mines offered few jobs for women, so she was able to stay in school for a long time, until she was fifteen, but the realities of working-class life finally caught up with her. Along the way the boys with whom she played went into the mines with their fathers.

> A child's labor added a small supplement to the family budget. A boy who might be our playmate one day would suddenly no longer be one of us; he would be a wage earner, with a role to play in his family and in society. But so many of them never reached manhood! . . . Many young miners . . . barely beyond childhood, lost their lives in mine accidents. . . .
>
> At fifteen I finished school. I was in poor health and not able to go to work. This meant an added burden for my family, which I was reluctant to impose on them. Since my good grades qualified me for further academic training, I decided to take the one-year preparatory course at the Teachers' Normal School and then the two-year

teacher-training course. After completing the first two years my adolescent dreams faded in the face of hard economic realities; books, food, clothes were all expenses my parents simply could not continue to meet. So I transferred to a dressmaking academy for two years. After this apprenticeship, I worked as a domestic [servant] for three years in the homes of local business men. At twenty-nine, seeking liberation from drudgery in other people's homes, I married a miner whom I had met during my first job as a domestic.

My mission in life was "fulfilled." I could not, ought not, aspire to more. Woman's goal, her only aspiration, had to be matrimony. . . .

Dolores Ibarruri with two of her children. For the working class, childhood was difficult.
Biblioteca Nacional, Madrid

A modern city: the Puerta del Sol, in the center of Madrid, in the 1890's. Biblioteca Nacional, Madrid

most skillful weavers. The average wage is about $3.58 per week. . . . The hours of work are 66 per week for the day and 48 for the night run. Three fourths of the cotton mills in Spain are now being operated night and day.

Eleven hours constitute the working day according to the law but several of the mills that I visited were running 12 hours. Work usually begins at 5:30 A.M. and ends at 6:30 P.M. with a half hour stop at 8:30 A.M. for breakfast and an hour and a half at noon for lunch.

Spain also developed heavy industry: coal mining and iron and steel production. These were located in the north, coal in Asturias and iron and steel in the Basque Provinces. These industries really got underway in the 1870's and were able to grow but never attained the levels of similar industries in Britain, France, or Germany.

The growth of modern industries brought with it the creation of a working class. These were people who owned no property and lived from selling their labor to the owners of the factories and mines. Some, especially in Catalonia, were former artisans whose trades had been killed off by industrialization, but most were migrants from the countryside. The workers were a relatively small percentage of the population, less than 20 percent of the work force in 1914, but because of their unions and political organizations they would have a disproportionate influence on national life.

Over the course of the nineteenth century Spain built a liberal political and social system basically similar to those elsewhere in Europe. But not all Spaniards were happy with that system. In the twentieth century their dissatisfactions, together with developments outside the country, would bring liberal Spain to a serious, and ultimately fatal, crisis.

The Crisis of Liberal Spain, 1898–1939

Dissatisfaction with the political, social, and economic arrangements of liberal Spain arose in the nineteenth century but did not yet represent a serious threat to the system. This changed in the twentieth century. Spain's humiliating defeat in the Spanish-American War was a major blow to the prestige and the legitimacy of the constitutional monarchy. Then, even though Spain remained neutral in World War I, the impact of the war was almost strong enough to lead to revolution, as it did in Russia in 1917. (See *The Land and People of the Soviet Union*.) Constitutional government was finally killed off in Spain, as it was in most of continental Europe between the two world wars, but only after a massive and complex three-year struggle known as the Spanish Civil War.

The Challengers

Liberal politics and liberal society in Spain were based on a number of basic principles: the legal equality of all citizens, the sanctity of private property, and a highly centralized, unitary state. By the end of the nineteenth century political movements had emerged that challenged one or more of these principles. In the twentieth century the most important challengers were the labor movement and regionalism.

There were some unions in Spain as early as the 1830's, but the organized labor movement and worker political movements did not really get underway until the 1860's and 1870's. From then on these movements were lasting, nationwide, and inspired by specific ideologies. Almost from the very beginning the labor left in Spain was divided between two competing movements, one based on Marxist socialism, the other based on anarchism.

Anarchism
Anarchism was the first of these to arrive in Spain, in 1868. Its strongholds were in Barcelona and among the landless laborers of the rural south. Until 1910 its history was one of repeated organization followed by repression. In 1910 anarchists created a lasting organization, the National Confederation of Labor (CNT). This grew rapidly during World War I, reaching 750,000 members by 1919. The CNT was banned between 1923 and 1930, and during this period it was taken over by radical elements. During the Second Republic (the First Republic had lasted only one year, from 1873 to 1874), after 1931, the CNT emerged once again and grew to have 1.5 million members.

Socialism
Socialism came to Spain in the 1870's, carried by Marx's son-in-law, Paul Lafargue. The Socialist Party (PSOE) was founded in 1879 by a printer named Pablo Iglesias (1850–1925). A so-

The Ideologies of the Labor Left

Until the Russian revolution of 1917 the two basic ideologies of the labor left were socialism and anarchism. Both criticized the industrial world that had begun to emerge in England at the end of the eighteenth century and in continental Europe during the nineteenth century. Both ideologies rejected private property in favor of some form of collective ownership, but beyond that they were very different.

Socialist ideology came from the work of Karl Marx and Friedrich Engels, who believed that history had laws that could be discovered through scientific study. (For more on socialism see *The Land and People of the Soviet Union*.) As they saw it, each economic and social system inevitably generated conflicts between classes. At a certain point these conflicts would lead to a revolution in which the ruling class would be overthrown. The bourgeoisie, industrialists and merchants, had already overthrown the feudal aristocracy. It would later be overthrown by another class, the workers of industrial society. Revolution could not happen at just any moment, but only when the existing economic system had developed to its full potential. For that

cialist union organization, the General Union of Workers (UGT) was created in 1888. The socialist organizations grew slowly but steadily, with few of the ups and downs experienced by the anarchists. Their real spurt came during the Second Republic, when the PSOE was the strongest political party in the country and the UGT came to have over 1 million members. The socialist strongholds were in Madrid and the mining zones of Vizcaya and Asturias. Only in the 1920's and 1930's did they win much support among agricultural laborers.

eventuality, the working class had to be organized politically.

Anarchism was developed by two Russian thinkers, Mikhail Bakunin (1814–1876) and Peter Kropotkin (1842–1921). It rejected not only private property but also the legitimacy of any one person having authority over another. This meant that it rejected not only the liberal state but the very idea of any state at all. Social organization could be the product only of voluntary cooperation. For example, anarchists rejected marriage as an institution because it put husbands in a position of authority over their wives. They advocated replacing it with what they called "free love," by which they meant long-term relationships between men and women based on equality and mutual respect, not sanctioned by outside authority.

Anarchists did not believe in laws of history that would determine when and where the revolution would take place. For them, it could take place at any time. They did not see the industrial working class as the most likely agent of revolution but looked instead to the people with the least stake in existing society, the landless peasantry. Finally, they rejected any participation in politics or the organization of political parties.

Regionalism   While the labor left challenged private property, regionalism challenged the extreme centralization of the liberal state. Regionalist movements emerged in the most advanced industrial regions of the country: Catalonia and the Basque Provinces. These were also parts of the country that had their own languages, Catalan and Basque respectively.

Catalonian regionalism began with the revival of Catalan as a literary language in the middle of the nineteenth century; it remained largely a cultural and intellectual movement until the end of the century. The loss to the United States of Spain's remaining American colonies in 1898 brought severe hardship to Catalonian industry, which lost its most important export markets. This led Catalonian industrialists to take up regionalism as a political movement, and in 1907 they created the Regionalist League, known as the Lliga, which was led by Francesc Cambó (1876–1947). The Lliga's major demand was for the creation of an autonomous regional government with power over matters such as education, cultural policy, and roads. There were also more radical regionalists who advocated complete independence from Spain.

Catalonian regionalism was led by the industrial elite and was self-consciously modern. The Basque regionalist movement, which was created by Sabino Arana at the end of the nineteenth century, was self-consciously antimodern. It was also, at least initially, blatantly racist, viciously attacking so-called *maketos*, Spaniards who moved to the region from other parts of the country. Basque regionalism sought to defend traditional Basque values, of which devout Catholicism was the most important, from the contamination of industrial society which was carried by those immigrants who did not speak Basque and who were not particularly religious.

The End of the Liberal Monarchy

After 1898 the challenge posed by the left and regionalism became stronger and more threatening. The year 1917 was almost a revolutionary year in Spain, as it was in Russia. Spain did not enter into World War I, but the war entered into Spanish life, causing massive inflation that led in turn to social and political protest. Army officers organized defense committees to demand pay increases and military reforms. Catalonian regionalists led a movement to democratize the political system. Socialists joined with other groups to demand a democratic republic through a general strike. Had these various protest movements come together, a revolution might have taken place. As it turned out, the Socialist strike frightened the army officers and the regionalists, who came to the support of the monarchy.

But the constitutional monarchy did not have long to live. Social protest continued and became much more violent, especially in Barcelona, where armed gangs, some supported by the unions and some by the employers, shot it out in the streets. Then, on June 23, 1921, at a place called Anual, the Spanish army in Morocco was almost wiped out by Moroccan tribesmen led by Abd-el-Krim. Of the fourteen thousand soldiers, ten thousand were killed. It later came out that King Alfonso XIII might have been directly responsible for the disaster. Shortly before a parliamentary commission was to issue its report on the subject, Alfonso backed a military coup by General Miguel Primo de Rivera.

As military dictators so often do, Primo promised to stay in power for only a brief time while he sorted out the mess caused by civilian politicians. And as military dictators so often do, he found that governing was much more complicated than he had thought. In the end, he stayed in power from September 1923 until January 1930 and fell only when a number of generals withdrew their support. The monarchy itself was badly stained by Alfonso's support of the dictatorship. Local elections held in April 1931 showed that most voters were opposed to the monarchy, and Alfonso stepped down. The monarchy was replaced by the Second Republic.

The Second Republic

From its beginning until November 1933 the Republic was governed by a coalition of Republican reformers and Socialists. During those two years the government legislated a number of major reforms intended to remove the most pressing dis-

The Importance of Agrarian Reform

Of all the problems with which the Republican-Socialist coalition government had to deal, the situation of the landless peasantry of Andalusia was the most urgent. In the south most of the land was held in the form of vast estates, which were owned by the very wealthy. Many people had very little land or none at all and depended on working as laborers on the large estates for their livelihood. There were far more people than there were jobs. This meant that wages were low and employers could pick and choose their workers. Hiring was usually done by a foreman in the town square. The following description, written by an anarchist, conveys the extent of the power landowners had over laborers and helps explain the recurrent social conflict in the region.

> The custom of hiring in the plaza was very profitable for the [landowner] and the foremen or managers because those who agreed to go to the field always saw the great number of their [acquaintances] who remained behind without work, and those who had work were submissive and allowed themselves to be easily exploited. If someone who was discontented complained, the foreman or manager responded arrogantly, with great show, "There are still men waiting in the plaza! Take a walk!" The one who complained was immediately dismissed and would lose the chance to work.

satisfactions created by liberalism. Catalonia was given an autonomous regional government. Laws were passed to improve the condition of workers, and an agrarian reform designed to relieve the misery of the landless peasantry of the south was implemented. The government also tried to reform the army and reduce the power of the Catholic church, especially in education.

This reform program antagonized many people. Some saw it as the equivalent of social revolution. The attack on the church angered many religious Spaniards who might not otherwise have opposed the government. On the other hand, for many Socialists the reforms were not sweeping enough. This caused the government coalition to fall apart. When elections were held in November 1933, they were won by a coalition of right-wing parties.

For the next two years this coalition set about reversing the reforms of the first two years. Labor legislation was ignored and land reform came to a halt. In the south landowners told unemployed workers that they could "Comed República," literally eat the Republic, if they were hungry.

The immediate result was to make unionists decide to take things into their own hands. In June 1934 the socialist agricultural workers' union called a general strike, which turned out to be a disastrous failure. Many Socialist Party politicians had also concluded that democracy was not working out as it should, and they began planning a revolution. They gave the signal for action in October 1934, but the movement was badly organized and quickly smothered by the government. The only exception came in Asturias, where the miners seized control of the coalfields and were able to resist 26,000 troops for two weeks before going down to defeat.

This pendulum from reform to reaction led to the radicalization of politics. Elections held in February 1936 were won by a broad coalition of reformists and Socialists known as the Popular Front. The new government found itself under strong pressure from its supporters to carry out sweeping reforms immediately. Peasants occupied land without waiting for legislation allowing them to do so. The spring of 1936 was a period of increasing political violence between left- and right-wing groups.

Much of the violence was due to a fascist party, the Falange, which grew during these months. The Falange was led by José Antonio Primo de Rivera (1903–1936), son of the dictator Miguel Primo de Rivera. Fascism was a radical right-wing political movement that emerged in Italy after World War I. It was based on extreme nationalism, a rejection of constitutional politics, and the use of violence against its enemies, especially socialists. (See *The Land and People of Italy*.)

The Spanish Civil War

While this was going on, a group of right-wing generals was planning a coup to overthrow the Popular Front government. On July 17, 1936, they struck. Resistance from parts of the army and from workers' militias defeated the coup in many parts of the country, but support from fascist Italy and Nazi Germany allowed the rebel generals to keep fighting. The coup turned into a civil war that lasted for nearly three years.

We usually think of civil wars as struggles between two clearly defined sides, such as the Union and the Confederacy in the United States Civil War. There were two such sides in the Spanish Civil War: the Republicans—those who favored the Popular Front and the reforms—and the Nationalists, as the rebels and their supporters were called. But each side had internal conflicts. These were more serious among the Republicans. The government had to deal with powerful worker organizations that did not always accept its authority as well as with pressure from a large number of political parties with very different objectives. The Republic's biggest problem was having to deal with the widespread social revolution which took place following the

Republican militiamen.   Biblioteca Nacional, Madrid

generals' coup attempt. Things were different in those areas under Nationalist control: It was a military dictatorship from the beginning, so political disputes were much more easily controlled.

Revolutionary Spain: Two Views

The military rebellion of July 17, 1936, touched off a spontaneous social revolution in much of Spain. In the countryside peasants occupied land; in the cities workers took control of their places of work. Throughout Republican territory the unions exercised power at the local level and, initially at least, controlled local government.

George Orwell (1903–1950), a British writer with left-wing political views, went to Barcelona at the end of 1936 and enrolled in the worker militia. He marveled at the sight of a city controlled by workers. He described what he saw, and his reactions to it, in his brilliant account of his time in Spain, *Homage to Catalonia*:

The aspect of Barcelona was something startling and overwhelming. It was the first time I had been in a town where the working class was in the saddle. Practically every building of any size had been seized by the workers and was draped with red flags or the red and black of the Anarchists. . . . Almost every church had been gutted and its images burnt. Churches here and there were being systematically destroyed by gangs of workmen. Every shop and cafe had an inscription saying that it had been collectivized. . . . Waiters and shop-walkers looked you in the face and treated you as an equal. . . . Tipping was forbidden by law. . . . There were no private motor cars, they had all been commandeered, and all the trams and taxis and much of the other transport were painted black and red. . . . It was the aspect of the crowds that was the queerest thing of all. In outward appearance it was a town in which the wealthy classes had practically ceased to exist. Except for a small number of women and foreigners there were no "well dressed" people at all. Practically everyone wore rough working class clothes, or blue overalls, or some variant of the militia uniform. All this was queer and moving. There was much in it I did not understand, in some ways I did not even like it, but I recognized it immediately as a state of affairs worth fighting for.

Fraser Lawton had another view of things. He was the manager of Barcelona Traction, Light and Power, an electricity and streetcar company owned by a Canadian firm headquartered in Toronto. He had lived in Barcelona for a number of years when the Civil War broke out. He found revolutionary Barcelona both repellent and frightening and described it in letters to his superior and to his daughter, Milly, both of whom were in London. Even though the two men had very different feelings about revolutionary Barcelona, they mentioned some of the same things and both captured the essence of revolution: that things had been turned upside down. Even clothing could not remain what it had been.

July 31, 1936

This morning . . . my car was held up for the first time by an armed group which is controlling traffic at that point. There was a rather amusing altercation between this group and my police escort, each one making the other show their credentials, but we were warned by them that we must drive past much slower on another occasion as we happened to be travelling rather quickly at the moment.

August 1, 1936

The [unions] occupy all the better hotels and the [Jockey] Club. The hotel we are at is a fourth rate place almost opposite the [Jockey] Club—we have to dine in the passage ways as they dare not put on the lights in the Restaurant . . . for fear that the occupants of the [Jockey] Club, the UGT, the Social[ist] syndicate, should fire at the guests. [There are] horrible women in men's overalls. I fear them more than all the men.

They are brutes and I went round the Ramblas today and to the Ritz. What a sight! What a mess! The town looks as though *en fête* [in carnival], but *en fête* with the revolutionaries and workmen to the fore—though quite a number of more decently dressed people, including women, are out again. . . . The whole city is a sight never to be forgotten—deplorable—awful—disgusting—a real taste of Russia. I should love to wander about more as the town is a sight, even if a depressing one.

August 8, 1936

No one wears hats now—men or women—and we are approaching the time when ties must go and then collars I suppose. The Ritz, Colon, Majestic, Ecuestre [hotels] are all crowded with the most awful riff raff and all the nice furniture must be ruined. . . . At the office the [unions] say what and who we may pay. . . . Black ruin!

International Brigades

The Spanish Civil War began as a purely Spanish conflict but foreigners quickly intervened, and this intervention was decisive as to the outcome. The two fascist dictatorships, Italy and Germany, provided massive military assistance to the

· 179 ·

Nationalists, who were led by Generalissimo Francisco Franco (1892–1975). The major democracies—Britain, France, and the United States—did not support the legitimately elected democratic government of the Republic. They were afraid to anger Germany's dictator, Adolf Hitler, and some saw the Popular Front government as close to communism, even though all the ministers were Republicans and the Communists were insignificant at the war's outset. The response of Britain and France was to organize the International Non-Intervention Agreement, but this was utterly ineffective. The fascist dictatorships signed the agreement but were allowed blatantly to ignore it and to go on providing Franco with help.

Only two countries helped the Republic: Mexico, which could not provide much assistance, and the Soviet Union. Soviet aid was channeled through the Spanish Communist Party and allowed it to become a major political force.

The Republic did receive other help from abroad, in the form of the International Brigades, 40,000 volunteers from twenty-five countries who went to Spain to fight. Among them were 3,200 Americans in what became known as the Abraham Lincoln Brigade. They went in the face of official opposition: The U.S. government refused to issue passports for Spain and they had to use excuses in order to get out of the country. Many claimed to be students traveling to France and then crossed the Spanish border surreptitiously. When they came back many were harassed by the government, which labeled them "premature anti-fascists."

Who were these volunteers and why did they go? Most of the North Americans and the English were workers who went to Spain because they saw the Civil War as part of a worldwide struggle between fascism and democracy. Many of the Europeans, especially the Germans and Italians, were already political refugees from dictatorships in their own countries. For them the Spanish conflict provided the next, and possibly the last, opportunity to defeat fascism.

Civil War: Image and Reality

This portrayal of the Civil War as a democratic crusade against international fascism led large numbers of artists and intellectuals to support the Republic in one way or another. Ernest Hemingway, John Dos Passos, and Paul Robeson were among the Americans. The most famous of those from other countries were George Orwell from England and André Malraux from France.

The Spanish reality that underlay the Civil War was much more complex. Franco was an old-fashioned, highly conservative general; he was not a fascist. On the other side, the Republic was a democratic regime with a democratically elected government, but by 1936 the anarchists and many Socialists, who were on the Republican side in the war, were fighting for revolution, not democracy. To make things even more complicated, the Communists, who gained in strength after the war began, were following orders from Stalin, who rightly feared Hitler and wanted an alliance with Britain and France, not to antagonize the western democracies. This meant that the Spanish Communist Party became the most determined opponent of the revolution that had taken place in the Republican zone and fought it by every means possible. The contrast between the simplistic interpretation of what was going on in Spain and the complex reality led many intellectuals to become disillusioned.

The Nationalists also explained the war in simplistic, global terms. Their cause was blessed by the Catholic church as a "crusade," and they described the war as a life-and-death struggle between Christian civilization and atheistic Communism. The Nationalists did not receive

Arriba
España

JUNTA DE BURGOS
LISBOA

Los Nacionales

A Republican poster portrays the Nationalists as the clergy supported by the army,
Fascist Italy, and Nazi Germany.   Archivo Histórico Nacional, Sección de la Guerra Civil,
Salamanca

many foreign volunteers, and hardly any intellectuals outside Spain supported them. They did have the support of many Catholics, of course, including Father Charles Coughlin, the popular right-wing American "radio priest" of the 1930's.

Here too reality was more complex. The conservative, Catholic French writer Georges Bernanos was in Majorca when the Civil War began. He saw very little that was Christian in the killing of political opponents that went on there and wrote a book denouncing the Nationalists. Yet in 1937, when the Nationalists conquered the Basque Provinces and they executed a number of priests who had supported the Republic, not even the Vatican protested.

From the military point of view the Spanish Civil War was an old-fashioned conflict. It resembled the First World War more than the Second. There was one major exception. With the Luftwaffe, the

Francisco Franco, center, at the battlefront.   Biblioteca Nacional, Madrid

German air force, using Spain as a practice field for new techniques, the Spanish Civil War was the first war in which air power played a major role.

Guernica   In particular it was the first war in which planes were used to bomb civilian targets. The major Republican cities, Madrid and Barcelona, were bombed regularly, but the most infamous episode took place elsewhere. On April 26, 1937, the Condor Legion of the German air force destroyed the Basque town of Guernica. For more than three hours German planes dropped bombs on an undefended town far behind the lines and of no military importance. The bombing of this Basque town inspired Pablo Picasso to create his most famous painting, *Guernica*.

The Republican war effort was debilitated by fierce internal political struggles. In May 1937 Barcelona was wracked by a number of days of armed conflict between government forces and anarchists. This led to the fall of the Republican government and the creation of a new one headed by Dr. Juan Negrín (1889–1956), a Socialist who had the support of the Communists. From this point on the Communists increased their political influence as well as their control over the army and the secret police. Their power was challenged only in the closing days of the war, when the commander of the Army of the Center, based in Madrid, staged a coup and established a Defense Committee that included members of a number of anti-Communist political forces. The Defense Committee tried to negotiate a peace with Franco, but he insisted on unconditional surrender.

Facing a better-equipped enemy and suffering from conflicts among its own supporters, the Republic had little chance of winning. It was almost a miracle that it held out as long as it did. Finally, on March 27, 1939, Nationalist troops entered Madrid. On April 1 Franco an-

Civilians rescue victims of Nationalist bombing of Barcelona in 1938.   Biblioteca Nacional, Madrid

nounced the end of the war. Half a million people had died; many thousands more fled abroad. Spain would not recover for twenty years.

Art and Culture

The first four decades of the twentieth century were a time of political and social crisis for Spain, but in the realm of culture they were a period of almost unprecedented brilliance. In these years, known as the Silver Age (a reference to the Golden Age of the seventeenth century), Spain produced some of its greatest artists.

Many of these artists drew their inspiration from the country's past, especially its folk traditions. This was most true in music. Classical composers such as Isaac Albéniz (1860–1909), Enrique Granados

(1867–1916), Manuel de Falla (1876–1946), Joaquín Turina (1882–1949), and Joaquín Rodrigo (1901–) based their works on popular and regional music. Only one notable Spanish composer, Roberto Gerhard, took any interest in the new atonal approach to music invented by the Viennese composer Arnold Schoenberg.

Such musical nationalism was quite common in Europe at this time, but the Spanish version made one important contribution to serious music, giving the guitar a status it had never enjoyed before. Until the latter part of the nineteenth century the guitar had not even had a standard physical form, and guitar players had had to write their own music. In the 1920's Andrés Segovia (1893–1987) set out to make the guitar a respected instrument, and all the leading Spanish composers wrote guitar music for him. Interest in the guitar then spread to Latin America and to the rest of Europe. Perhaps the most famous music composed for the guitar is Rodrigo's *Concierto de Aranjuez.*

Gaudí

The work of Antonio Gaudí (1852–1926), Spain's greatest modern architect, was a unique and bizarre combination of many influences. These included oriental and Islamic motifs, Art Nouveau, and the forms of the natural world. This interest in natural forms dominates Guell Park in Barcelona, which was intended as a luxury housing development. Only three of the houses were built, and today it is a public park. The most important influence on Gaudí was medieval Gothic architecture. This is evident in Gaudí's most outstanding work, the still-unfinished Church of the Holy Family in Barcelona, to which he dedicated most of the last thirty years of his life.

Gaudí's work is considered to be among the most original—and strange—in twentieth-century architecture, but despite his undoubted genius Gaudí was an architectural dead end. He had little influence inside Spain and none outside it.

Artists Abroad   It was in the visual arts, where they were in the vanguard, that Spanish artists would have their greatest international success. Here a group of Spaniards—Juan Gris (1887–1927), Joan Miró (1893–1983), Salvador Dalí (1904–1989), and above all Pablo Picasso (1881–1973)—figure among the very greatest painters of the twentieth century.

All four shared the experience of living in Paris, then the cultural capital of the western world, and being exposed there to the most advanced trends in painting. The art world was in a ferment at the end of the nineteenth century, and new approaches and methods were being invented continually. In 1907 Picasso, along with the Frenchman

Gaudí's Church of the Holy Family remains unfinished.   Paul A. McDonough

Georges Braque, created a new style called Cubism. This was a new technique for representing physical objects. It consisted of mentally dissecting objects, usually everyday things such as guitars, and then graphically reassembling the fragments into a picture. Cubists were concerned with the structure of things and deliberately made little use of color.

Picasso was not just a founder of Cubism. He was without question the dominant figure in the visual arts in the first half of the twentieth century. This position came from his constant experiments with new styles and his interest in a wide range of themes.

The horrendous slaughter of World War I led many artists and intellectuals to question the rationalism on which European society was based. Surrealism was the most important of the artistic movements that emerged in the 1920's. Surrealists believed that reality was not orderly or logical and that true knowledge could be achieved only by liberating the creative powers of the unconscious and of dreams.

Melting Watches
Miró is considered by art critics the greatest of the Surrealist painters, but Dalí was much more famous. Dali's fame was due more to his extravagant personality and his flair for publicity than to his art. At one point Dalí even made television commercials for Chrysler. Late in his life he set up his own museum in his hometown. After his death it also became his mausoleum, and plans were developed to build "Cosmo Dalí," a holiday resort and amusement park.

The newest, and most widely popular, form of the visual arts was the movies. Here too Spain produced one of the world's most outstanding artists, although he did very little of his work in Spain.

Luís Buñuel (1900–1983) studied science at the University of Madrid but was friends with Dalí and the poet and dramatist Frederico

Salvador Dalí's The Persistence of Memory. *1931. Oil on canvas, 9½ x 13".*
Collection, The Museum of Modern Art, New York. Given anonymously.

García Lorca. He began to work in movies in Paris in 1925 and he made his first movie there in 1928. *An Andalusian Dog*, which he wrote with Dalí, was the first Surrealist movie. The first film he made in Spain was *Land Without Bread* (1933), a documentary about one of the most backward regions of the country. It was banned by the government and was not shown in Spain until the Civil War. After 1936 he spent most of his life abroad, in the United States, Mexico, and France, and made his films there. Throughout his long career his movies constantly criticized the bourgeoisie and the Catholic church.

A New Generation of Writers

In literature, as in the visual arts, the early twentieth century saw a reaction against realism and the rule of reason. The aim of writing was less and less to portray reality; instead, writers sought to deal with the individual's relation to the world. The subject was no longer what was seen but what was felt by the viewer. In large part this approach emerged from the profound

Joan Miró's The Beautiful Bird Revealing the Unknown to a Pair of Lovers. *1941. Gouache and oil wash on paper, 18 x 15".* Collection, The Museum of Modern Art, New York. Acquired through the Lillie P. Bliss Bequest.

dissatisfaction many writers felt about modern society, which was perceived to be too materialistic and too little concerned with beauty and the spirit.

Novelists paid less attention to character and plot than to technique. They were especially interested in revising the role of the narrator. For example in *Mist*, the author, Miguel de Unamuno, also became a character, debating with the protagonist Augusto Pérez, the question of whether a fictional character can act without the permission of the author.

In poetry the first new movement was modernism. This had foreign origins, in the works of the Nicaraguan Rubén Darío and the Frenchman Paul Verlaine. For the modernists, the poet's role was to provide beauty to a world that lacked it, to describe things of beauty in order to capture the sensations they stimulated. In the hands of Spanish poets, such as Antonio Machado (1875–1939), modernist techniques produced melancholy and introspective verses. Machado's contemporary Juan Ramón Jiménez (1881–1958) won the Nobel Prize for Literature in 1956.

The next generation of writers, known as the Generation of 1927, produced a number of outstanding poets. They drew on a large number of sources for inspiration, from contemporary experiments in other countries to the literary traditions of their own country, and especially the seventeenth-century poet Luís de Góngora, and from folklore and popular culture.

One member of this generation, Vicente Aleixandre (1898–1984), won the Nobel Prize in 1977, but by far the most famous, especially outside Spain, was Federico García Lorca (1898–1936). García Lorca's fame is due in large part to his early death. Executed by the Nationalists in the first months of the Civil War, he became a symbol of the death of art and free expression at the hands of fascism.

García Lorca's early poetry drew most heavily on Andalusian, and es-

Federico García Lorca: A Spanish Poet in New York

García Lorca made his first trip outside Spain in 1929. He went to New York and stayed for nine months. Life in such a huge city was a new experience for him, and he did not like it much. He was intrigued by blacks, and especially their culture, and distressed by what he saw of racial discrimination. The first poems he wrote while in New York were about blacks.

García Lorca's *Poet in New York*, which was not published until after his death, is a condemnation of modern urban society and the spiritual emptiness it produced. His dark vision is shown in the following poem, "Dawn."

> *Dawn in New York has*
> *four columns of mire*
> *and a hurricane of black pigeons*
> *splashing in the putrid waters.*

pecially Gypsy, folklore. His symbolism is always difficult to decipher.

García Lorca was also a playwright, and in the 1930's he devoted more of his energy to his plays than to his poetry. His greatest plays—*Blood Wedding*, *Yerma*, and *The House of Bernarda Alba*—drew on Andalusian folklore and small-town life. They dealt with the effects of the suppression of instinct by social codes and the special suppression of women.

Dawn in New York groans
on enormous fire escapes
searching between the angles
for spikenards of drafted anguish.

Dawn arrives and no one receives it in his mouth
because morning and hope are impossible there:
sometimes the furious swarming coins
penetrate like drills and devour abandoned children.

Those who go out early know in their bones
there will be no paradise or loves that bloom and die:
they know they will be mired in numbers and laws,
in mindless games, in fruitless labors.

The light is buried under chains and noises
in an impudent challenge to rootless science.
And crowds stagger sleeplessly through the boroughs
as if they had just escaped a shipwreck of blood.

García Lorca saw the theater as important to national life. During the Second Republic he was involved in La Barraca, a traveling theater company made up mostly of students, which took classic Spanish plays to villages that had not had the opportunity to see them before. This idea was every bit as experimental as the most experimental writing of the time. With the Nationalist victory in the Civil War, all forms of cultural innovation were brought to a bloody end.

From Franco to Felipe, 1939–1989

Francisco Franco ruled Spain as *"El Caudillo* [The Leader] by the Grace of God" from the end of the Civil War until his death in November 1975. The thirty-six years of the regime offer at least two paradoxes. Franco sought to impose a very clear and narrow view of what Spain was on his country, but by the time he died it was more diverse than ever. Franco wanted a nonconstitutional, dictatorial form of government to survive him, but within three years of his death Spain had a democratic, constitutional government, and few people were unhappy with the change.

There were a number of reasons for these paradoxical outcomes. The most important was the rapid economic development that took place after 1960. Along with this economic development came sweeping social change. By 1970 Spaniards were much more prosperous than they had been before. They were also increasingly demanding the political and cultural liberties that they knew went with economic prosperity in the rest of western Europe. The desire for political change was shared by significant elements of the country's elites. For industrialists and financiers the continued existence of the Franco regime was a threat to social stability and continued economic growth. For King Juan Carlos, Franco's hand-picked successor as head of state, political change was the only way to legitimatize his position and to avoid violence.

"One, Great, and Free"

Franco wanted to create a Spain based on Catholicism, extreme centralization, and the preservation of social order. This program was known as National Catholicism.

The first step in achieving this new order was to eliminate those organizations that had an alternative vision of Spain. The purge began during the Civil War itself. All left-wing political parties and trade unions that supported the Republic were banned. Individual men and women, known generically as "reds," were brought to trial and sent to prison camps or executed. A frequently cited estimate for the number of people killed by the Nationalists for political reasons during the war is two hundred thousand, although other historians have suggested lower figures. Whatever the exact number, there can be no doubt that the scale of such executions was massive.

The repression continued after 1939. About two hundred thousand more were executed or died of disease in concentration camps between 1939 and 1943. The Valley of the Fallen, Franco's massive monument to those who died during the Civil War, was built largely by the forced labor of political prisoners. Strikes were prohibited. A law passed in

1940 made it a crime to belong to a Communist or Masonic organization or to spread ideas that threatened the Catholic faith, the institutions of the state, or social harmony. After 1953 this law was applied by special military courts.

The political diversity of the Republic, and even the liberal monarchy, was replaced by a single, official party, and government-run trade unions. In April 1937 Franco merged the various political groups that supported his rebellion into the National Movement. Three years later the National Union Organization was created.

All Republican legislation that violated the new regime's vision was repealed. The most important areas of reaction were regional autonomy, religion, and land reform.

The motto of Franco's Spain was "One, Great, and Free." The order of the words was no accident. No reform passed by the Republic angered the military more than the granting of regional autonomy to Catalonia in 1932. (The Basque Provinces were given autonomy shortly after the Civil War began.) To army officers even the most timid decentralization threatened the disintegration of the fatherland.

Franco revoked Catalonian and Basque autonomy immediately. The regime made it a crime to use the Basque and Catalan languages in schools, in newspapers, or on the radio, and the names of streets and towns were put into Castilian.

Catholicism was made the official religion of the state. All education had to conform to Catholic beliefs, and religious education was compulsory at all levels. Civil marriage was prohibited. Bishops sat in the Francoist parliament. In 1953 the regime signed a Concordat, or treaty, with the Vatican leaving the Church freer from state interference than at any time since the early eighteenth century.

The regime reversed the Republic's agrarian reform and returned to the previous landowners the land that had been distributed before the war. Landowners in the south went even further, taking advantage of the political situation to evict tenants and sharecroppers, including Nationalist supporters, in order to cultivate the land themselves. The wages of agricultural laborers fell, and a more demanding workday was imposed. Laborers could not resist these changes, and for almost twenty years there was little opportunity to move elsewhere. That unfavorable situation changed in the 1960's.

Culture

The Franco years comprised a break in the cultural development of Spain. Many of the country's outstanding cultural figures were in exile after the war, and the regime practiced sweeping censorship of all forms of artistic activity. From 1938 to 1966 all books, magazines, and newspapers had to be submitted to government censors for approval before they could be published.

Censored! Censorship had a significant effect on literature. Until the mid-1950's the most important form of novel was the apolitical description of society. Among the best of these were *Five Hours with Mario* by Miguel Delibes (1920–), *Jarama* by Rafael Sánchez Ferlosio (1927–), and *Time of Silence* by Luís Martín Santos (1925–1964), but the best known internationally were *The Family of Pascual Duarte* and *The Beehive* by Camilo José Cela (1916–). Both these books had trouble with Franco's censors—which is ironic, since Cela himself had once worked as a government censor. This did not prevent him from winning the Nobel Prize for Literature in 1989.

Before a movie could be made, the script had to pass the censor; however, a list of banned subjects was not published until 1963. That list included divorce, abortion, euthanasia, birth control, adultery, prostitution, and illicit sexual behavior. Nudes were not allowed until 1975.

From 1941 on all foreign-language films had to be dubbed so that the dialogue could be changed when necessary. The most famous incident involved *Mogambo*, a movie made by American director John Ford in 1954. In the film a married woman, played by Grace Kelly, on safari with her husband, has an affair with the guide, played by Clark Gable. To prevent Spaniards from being exposed to adultery on the screen, the censors turned the husband and wife into brother and sister, even though they slept in the same tent.

Television was introduced in 1954, but until the 1980's there were only two channels, and both were owned by the state.

Censorship came to an end only in 1977, two years after Franco's death, but it had been relaxed in the 1960's in an attempt to improve Spain's international image. Marxist and other prohibited books became available, and periodicals published in Catalan were allowed. Even so, censorship remained unpredictable: In 1968 the popular singer Joan Manuel Serrat was prohibited from taking part in the Eurovision song contest because he planned to sing in Catalan.

The Economic Miracle

Three years of civil war left Spain devastated. Half a million people died; another half million were in exile. Almost half of the country's railroad equipment was destroyed. Agriculture was far below prewar levels.

The Franco regime initially applied policies of economic self-sufficiency and massive governmental intervention in the economy; these were copied from those used by Benito Mussolini in Italy. Over twenty years these failed to rebuild the Spanish economy, and by 1959 the country was on the verge of bankruptcy. This crisis led to a major

Millions fled the countryside and villages such as Huecija, in Almería, during the 1960's.   Courtesy of the Tourist Office of Spain

change in policy. Government intervention was reduced, and Spain became more integrated into the western European and North American economy. These changes helped create what is known as the Spanish "economic miracle." From 1960 to 1974 the Spanish economy grew more rapidly than any in the world except that of Japan.

The Spanish miracle depended on three outside forces. First, the opening of the economy encouraged foreigners to invest in Spain. Between 1960 and 1970 foreigners invested $650 million. Almost half came from the United States.

A second major source of capital was the remittances sent back by emigrants. The Spanish government encouraged, and even subsidized, emigration to countries that needed unskilled workers. The two million Spaniards who left between 1960 and 1976 joined large numbers of Portuguese, Italians, Yugoslavs, and Turks as "guest workers" in

France, West Germany, and Switzerland. In 1973 they sent back to their families in Spain over $1 billion.

The final external force driving Spain's development was tourism. North Americans and people from the wealthier European countries were drawn to Spain in the millions by the beautiful beaches, hot weather, and bargain prices. Tourism quickly became Spain's largest industry.

After the "economic miracle" industry and services played a larger role in the economy than did agriculture. This was a significant change: In 1960 42 percent of all Spanish workers were in agriculture; by 1975 only 23 percent were. Landless laborers left the south for opportunities in Spain's growing cities or abroad. Small farmers abandoned the land in droves for the glamour and affluence of the cities. Almost 6 million Spaniards moved from one province to another between 1962 and 1976.

These economic changes brought sweeping, almost revolutionary, social changes. Rural life lost all its prestige, especially among young people. Farmers' sons refused to take land in inheritance, and many younger farmers were unable to find wives. Entire villages were abandoned. In 1984 one newspaper reported that there were more than 2,000 abandoned villages and 3,500 more that were nearly uninhabited.

Educational opportunities increased after 1960 as the public-school system was extended dramatically. Until then, the regime had allowed the Church to play a dominant role in education, but the demands of a rapidly changing economy demanded a better-educated population. The number of students in high school grew from 260,000 in 1953 to 1.5 million in 1970, and the percentage of high school students in public schools tripled between 1960 and 1975. University education also became much more accessible. In 1940 there were only 37,000 university students in Spain; by 1980 there were 650,000.

Not all traditional pastimes have disappeared: a game of petanco *in a city park, 1985.*
Sergio Purtell

Consumerism

Spain entered the world of consumerism with a vengeance. At the end of the 1950's basic necessities consumed 82 percent of the average Spaniard's income; by 1974 they ate up only 68 percent. At the same time, average annual income jumped from $290 to $2,500. Spaniards had a lot more money left for luxuries, and they spent it—on household appliances, on stereos, on televisions, on cars, and even on holidays abroad.

Spaniards increasingly rejected local and traditional culture in favor of an international culture. Soccer, which was used by the Franco regime as a stimulus to patriotism, displaced bullfighting as the national passion. The real leaders in this cultural change were young people. They threw themselves into an international youth culture based above all on rock music. Spain had its own domestic bands, including Los Bravos, whose "Black Is Black" was an international hit, but foreigners were dominant. The Beatles, the Rolling Stones, and the rest of the British wave of the mid-1960's reached Spain only shortly after the rest of Europe.

A series of singers, the most famous of whom were Joan Manuel Serrat, Luis Llach, and Raimon, combined rock and folk music with political protest as Bob Dylan and Joan Baez did in the United States.

The Changing Place of Women

Among the changes that Spain experienced none was more sweeping than that in the place of women. Through the nineteenth century and until the Civil War, the position of women in Spain was about the same as it was in North America and elsewhere in western Europe. Women were not equal to men. Their only legitimate aspiration in life was marriage and the management of the home. Respectable women could apply these domestic virtues outside the home, for example in charitable activities, but they were not expected to engage in other types of public activity. In the eyes of the law married women were extensions of their husbands and barely people in their own right. This had changed with the Republic, which made women more or less the legal equals of men.

The Franco regime turned back the clock for women. Married women were made once again into legal subordinates of their husbands. The sexual double standard was embodied in the law: A father could legally kill his unmarried daughter if he caught her engaged in a sexual act. The Labor Charter promised to take married women out of the work force. Married women could not work without their husbands' permission.

The most extreme of these provisions were eliminated in the early

1960's, but the legal position of Spanish women remained much worse than that of women in many other European countries. Full equality came only with the return to democracy. The Constitution of 1978 and later laws prohibited discrimination on the grounds of gender and made wives equal to their husbands within the family. Divorce was legalized in 1981 and abortion two years later.

Teens in Franco's Spain

In Franco's Spain the world of women, and especially their contacts with men, was severely restricted. Coeducation was banned. Courtship was very tightly controlled; it took place in public and collectively. Dating was unknown. The first stage of courtship was a ritual known as the *paseo*, the promenade. Novelist Carmen Martín Gaite (1925–) was born and grew up in Salamanca, a small and very conservative provincial capital. Below she describes what it was like to be a teenaged girl in Spain in the 1940's, 1950's, and into the 1960's.

In every Spanish city there was a main street or square where the now obsolete ceremony of the promenade took place at fixed times. From one to two in the afternoon and nine to ten at night groups of girlfriends got together to go for a walk and, arm in arm, studying the boys, both those they knew and those they did not, more or less openly and talking quietly about them, promenaded peacefully and unimaginatively. . . . In the main square of Salamanca the girls walked clockwise and the boys counter-clockwise. Since both groups walked at about the same, generally slow, pace you knew that for each lap around the square, you would have two opportunities to see the person with whom you wanted to exchange glances and you could even calculate with a fair degree of accuracy just where the fleeting encounter would occur. . . . If a group of boys approached a group of girls so that a member of one could "accompany" a member of the other they always changed direction to walk with the girls; they never made the girls walk in the same direction as them.

Young people stroll around the Plaza Mayor in Salamanca, about 1970. Angel
Esteban Martín

Of course, young people did what they could to find ways of being alone together. The movies offered one opportunity, but even that was far from perfect:

A girl never went to the movies alone, just as she never entered a cafe alone. Going to the movies was a group ritual. . . . If the boy who was "accompanying" a specific girl who was a member of the group found out that they were going to the movies together the next day he might let slip the suggestion that they leave a ticket for him at the entrance because he also wanted to see that movie and this way they could see it together. . . . Although even their elbows barely touched just having that masculine physical presence so near created illusions of intimacy, especially when the movie was a love story. Holding hands, the first liberties taken by a couple, did not even enter anyone's mind in those days, unless it was the mind of an unusually daring boy. . . . The authorities were concerned about the possibility of immorality in the cinemas and in some provinces they took measures which recalled the Inquisition. . . . In Almendralejo, when cinema employees observed improper behavior they projected onto the screen a warning to "the occupants of row such and such," not mentioning the seat numbers but with the threat to do so if they did not behave.

Spain in the World

The changes in Franco's economic policies coincided with a change in Spain's international position. Immediately after the Second World War Spain was isolated from the rest of the western world. In the eyes of the United States and the other Europeans Franco was little more than a fascist dictator. For ten years Spain was left out of the United Nations and was not invited to participate in the Marshall Plan, under which the United States provided massive investments for the rebuilding of Europe.

Spain's isolation began to recede in the early 1950's. Franco had always argued that he was an anti-Communist. Spain had remained neutral during the war, and its only military contribution had been to send a volunteer force, known as the Blue Division, to fight against the Soviet Union. With the outbreak of the Cold War Franco's anti-Communist posture struck a responsive chord in Washington, and in 1953 Spain and the United States signed the Bases Treaty. This gave the United States the right to maintain three air bases and one naval base on Spanish soil in return for cash payments. Two years later Spain became a member of the United Nations.

The Europeans were less forgiving than the Americans. The United States proposed Spain for membership in the North Atlantic Treaty Organization (NATO), but the other members of the alliance refused. After all, they said, the North Atlantic Treaty of April 4, 1949, de-

Francisco Franco greets President Dwight D. Eisenhower during his visit to Spain in December 1959. AP/Wide World Photos

clared that NATO was based on the principles of "democracy, individual liberty, and the rule of law," and those words did not describe Franco's Spain. The European Economic Community (EEC—which has since evolved into the European Community, or EC) took a similar line. When Franco applied for admission in 1962, he was told that only countries with freely elected, democratic governments would be considered.

The Transition

Unlike most dictators, Franco worked hard to make sure that the regime continued after his death. In 1947 he declared Spain a monarchy. He then named Prince Juan Carlos (1938–   ), the grandson of Alfonso XIII, heir to the throne and took charge of his education. The appointment of his close collaborator Admiral Luís Carrero Blanco (1903–1973) as Prime Minister in 1973 left things, as Franco put it, "well tied up."

But Franco's plan unraveled quickly. In December 1973 the Basque separatist organization ETA (Basque Land and Liberty) assassinated Carrero Blanco in the center of Madrid. Social and political protest increased dramatically: In 1975 there were more than 3,100 strikes, including many in public services such as the post office and the Madrid subway. Early in 1976 the government had to call in the army to run the subway trains. Faced with such massive evidence of popular unrest, the economic elite, and some figures within the regime, came to see that dictatorship no longer made sense in an advanced and complex society. Juan Carlos, the heir to the throne, agreed and decided that his monarchy had to be a democratic one if it were to last.

Franco had been on the verge of death for months, kept alive by the most modern life-support technology available. After his death the

Juan Carlos I: King of All the Spaniards

The Law of Succession of 1947 declared that Spain was a monarchy, but Franco did not immediately decide on who would become king after his death. The person with the strongest case was Juan de Borbón, the oldest son of Alfonso XIII, but he was too liberal for Franco's tastes. Following a series of negotiations, Franco agreed to make Juan's son, Juan Carlos (1938–), heir to the throne, but only on condition that the boy, and his education, be put into Franco's hands.

In the twenty-seven years that he was under Franco's tutelage Juan Carlos never gave any indication of having a mind of his own. As a result, most Spaniards saw him as very much the creature of Franco and they expected that he would retain the Francoist political system. The difficult circumstances in which he came to the throne after Franco's death led some people to give him the nickname Juan Carlos "the Brief."

Juan Carlos came to the throne determined to be the "king of all the Spaniards," as he said during the coronation ceremony. This determination, combined with the skill of leading politicians in the regime and the opposition, as well as the amazing political maturity of the Spanish people, made possible the transition to democracy. The transition is all the more impressive because it was made in the midst of an extended economic recession touched off by the petroleum crisis of 1973.

The success of the Spanish transition made it a model for people in countries such as Argentina and Brazil, which emerged from military dictatorships in the early 1980's, and then for some people in central and eastern Europe following the collapse of the Communist regimes there in 1989.

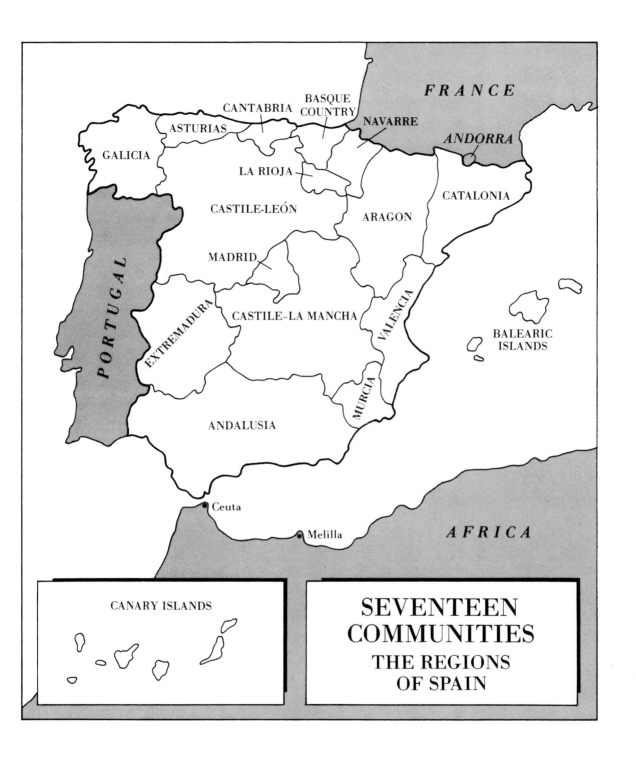

FRANCE

GALICIA

ASTURIAS

CANTABRIA

BASQUE COUNTRY

NAVARRE

ANDORRA

LA RIOJA

CATALONIA

CASTILE-LEÓN

ARAGON

PORTUGAL

MADRID

EXTREMADURA

CASTILE–LA MANCHA

VALENCIA

BALEARIC ISLANDS

MURCIA

ANDALUSIA

Ceuta

Melilla

AFRICA

CANARY ISLANDS

SEVENTEEN COMMUNITIES
THE REGIONS OF SPAIN

American comedy show *Saturday Night Live* regularly ran satirical news bulletins stating "This just in, Generalissimo Francisco Franco is still dead." His death was announced on November 20, 1975. He probably died earlier, but the announcement was delayed so that it could coincide with the anniversary of the death of the regime's martyr José Antonio Primo de Rivera, who had been executed by the Republic on November 20, 1936. Many Spaniards cried when they heard the news; but others partied, and by the end of the day there was no champagne left in the stores of Madrid.

Less than two years after Franco died, Spain held democratic elections. This remarkable and unprecedented transition took place peacefully. Adolfo Suárez (1932–), who had held a number of important positions within the Franco regime, was named Prime Minister and negotiated a political reform with the leaders of the opposition. Both his political skill and their realism were essential. Elections were held in June 1977, and a new Constitution, also a product of negotiation, was approved in December 1978. The Constitution made Spain a fully democratic country. It also recognized Spain's diversity, creating a state of autonomous regions somewhat similar to the federal system of the United States.

The King Chooses Democracy
Suárez won the first two democratic elections, but he resigned unexpectedly at the beginning of 1981. On February 23, 1981, as parliament was voting to appoint his successor, a group of Civil Guards broke into the building and took the deputies hostage. At the same time military units in Valencia also rose against the government. This attempted military coup failed, in large part because of the refusal of the King, who is also commander-in-chief of the armed forces, to go along. The leaders of the coup were tried in 1982 and sent to prison, although only the two top leaders were given long sentences.

Former president Adolfo Suárez, left, comes to the aid of Vice President Gutiérrez Mellado, who is being roughed up by Civil Guards who invaded the parliament building during the attempted coup of February 23, 1981. AP/Wide World Photos

The events of February 23, 1981, were the greatest challenge to Spain's new democratic system. Spaniards showed their commitment to democracy a few days later by participating in massive marches. In Madrid more than a million people took part. If any further proof of popular opinion was necessary, it came with the election of October 28, 1982. The Socialist Party, led by a handsome young labor lawyer, Felipe González (1942–), won the largest electoral victory in Spanish history. Felipe, as he is popularly called, again led his party to majorities in subsequent elections in June 1986 and October 1989.

Spain Today

Since 1960 Spain has changed rapidly to become more like the rest of western Europe. The economic miracle made Spain a more urban, industrialized society. It also made it one of the most prosperous countries in the world. These economic changes brought significant social change with them. Then, after the death of Franco in 1975, Spain returned to political democracy. Taken together these changes have made Spain much more like the rest of the western world than it had been for at least two hundred years.

Spain in the World

For most of the twentieth century Spain was on the sidelines of major international events. It was neutral in the two world wars and then, under Franco, was largely isolated internationally. This situation has now changed dramatically, as a democratic Spain has finally been welcomed into two of the major international organizations of the western world.

Spain joined NATO in June 1982 and confirmed its membership in a referendum held in March 1986. The referendum also established the main condition for Spain remaining in NATO: the withdrawal of United States forces from the bases they had occupied in Spain since 1953.

Spain finally entered the European Community (EC) in January 1986. Since then Spanish Prime Minister, Felipe González, has been one of the strongest advocates within the EC for further unification, political as well as economic. The Spanish public has also developed a strong European identity: a poll taken by Spanish and British media at the end of 1989 showed that Spaniards had a more positive view of the EC and were far more supportive of further unification than the French, English, or Germans.

Spain has also become more active beyond the boundaries of Europe. It has provided economic assistance to some Latin American countries and has sought to establish itself as the bridge between Latin America and the EC. These initiatives have not always been well received. In particular, many Latin Americans have been annoyed by the way in which Spain planned to celebrate the five hundredth anniversary of Columbus's voyage of 1492: They found it too much of a glorification of conquest and colonialism for their taste.

In the summer of 1990 through March 1991 Spain participated in the military operations in the Gulf prompted by the Iraqi invasion of Kuwait. And in October 1990, during a visit by Soviet President Mikhail Gorbachev to Madrid, Felipe González announced that Spain would be providing the Soviet Union with $1.8 billion in economic aid.

Spain's new place in the world can also be seen in the range of activities in which Spaniards are influential or famous at the international level. A list of such people would include architect and urban planner Ricardo Bofill, International Olympic Committee President Juan Antonio Samaranch, opera singers Plácido Domingo and Montserrat Caballé, pianist Alicia de Larrocha, singer Julio Iglesias, movie director Pedro de Almodóvar, tennis player Arantxa Sánchez Vicario, and

The Unification of Europe

Shortly after World War II a number of the major countries of western Europe began to create institutions, such as the European Coal and Steel Community, for economic cooperation. On March 25, 1957, six countries—Belgium, France, Italy, Luxembourg, the Netherlands, and West Germany—signed the Treaty of Rome, which created the European Economic Community. The objectives of the Community were to remove trade barriers; coordinate agricultural, economic, and transportation policies; and make possible the free flow of labor and capital. Denmark, Ireland, and the United Kingdom joined in 1973, Greece joined in 1981, and Portugal and Spain joined in 1986.

The scope of integration became wider in the 1980's. In 1987 the members signed the Single European Act, which increased the power of the European Parliament and eliminated the ability of any single member to veto decisions made by the Council of Ministers. The European Monetary System, which linked the currencies of the member states, was also strengthened. This meant that national governments had less control over their monetary policy. The ongoing trend toward greater integration will mean that national governments will lose more of their autonomy to Community institutions. Some countries, especially Great Britain, have found this difficult to accept, but Spain has not.

Tennis star Arantxa Sánchez Vicario.   Andrew P. Long/SportsLight

golfers José María Olazábal and Severiano Ballesteros.

There are also a number of Spanish athletes who are famous in Europe and beyond, but not in the United States, because the sports in which they participate are not popular here. These include cyclists Miguel Indurain and Pedro Delgado, soccer player Emilio Buitragueño, and motorcycle racer Carlos Pons.

The Internationalization of Culture

In recent decades Spain has become a consumer society. This means that Spaniards can now acquire all the items that define the "good life" of the west: telephones, televisions, CD players, videos, and, above all, cars. There are also less tangible forms of consumerism: More and more Spaniards take vacations abroad, and to destinations that are becoming more and more exotic—and expensive. They also spend much time, and large amounts of money, studying English. There are large numbers of private language schools, but more recently residential language programs for young people—primarily in England and Ireland but also in the United States, at prices around $3,000 per month—have become popular. Middle- and upper-class Spaniards have now begun to send their teenaged children to attend a year of school abroad, usually in the United States or Britain.

The rise of consumerism means more than just more people buying more things. There has also been a significant change in cultural values. Urban employment and urban living have become everyone's goal, while rural life is for losers. Until the 1930's Spaniards of all classes strove to acquire land; since 1960 they have raced to abandon it. The change from a society in which farming was prestigious to one in which prestige is found in the urban world is summed up in an advertisement for an agricultural college in the bus station in Salamanca, part of the country's agricultural heartland: "To be a farmer is a profession, not a life sentence."

Those young people who remain in villages are uninterested in local traditions, such as processions and folklore. Their attention is drawn instead to commercialized, urban culture, especially movies, rock music, and sports.

Spanish teenagers are avid participants in the international rock culture. All the major stars pass through Madrid and Barcelona on their international tours. In the summer of 1988 young Spaniards flocked to see Michael Jackson and Bruce Springsteen as well as the Amnesty International tour headlined by Sting. When Madonna and her "Blond Ambition" tour went to Madrid and Barcelona in July 1990, it was front-page news, even in the most sophisticated newspapers in the country. Her Barcelona concert was broadcast live on national television.

The NBA in Spain

Soccer has displaced bullfighting as the most popular sporting event. First-division teams fill their stadia, some of which can seat over 100,000 people; weekly sports magazines outsell the regular daily press, and many millions of dollars are wagered on the weekly pools every year.

Since 1980 basketball has become increasingly popular too. Spain's silver medal at the 1984 Olympics in Los Angeles stimulated a major jump in the sport's popularity. Spaniards now pay considerable attention to the NBA, as well as to their own league, where some Americans play. Spanish television has broadcast every round of the NBA finals in recent years. The new status of basketball was confirmed in October 1988, when Real Madrid hosted an invitational tournament that fea-

Boston Celtics star Larry Bird presents Prince Felipe, heir to the throne, with his jersey, in 1988. NBA Photos/Andrew Bernstein

tured the Boston Celtics. The tournament was repeated in 1990, with Barcelona and the New York Knicks in the leading roles. When the World League of American Football started up in March 1991, one of the teams was from Barcelona.

The sponsorship of these tournaments reveals another facet of the internationalization of culture: In both 1988 and 1990 the basketball sponsor was McDonald's. Spaniards frequently say that Madrid was the first city in Europe to have all the major American burger chains—McDonald's, Burger King, and Wendy's—although it is not clear whether they say this with pride or embarrassment. The food is identical to that in the United States, but some concessions are made to local tastes and customs—for example, in Spain you can get wine or beer with your Big Mac.

New Shopping Hours

Eating habits are not the only ones that are changing. So are shopping habits. Shopping hours in Spain have long been closely regulated, both by custom and by law. Shops would open at nine-thirty or ten in the morning, close for the traditional long lunch from one-thirty to four-thirty, and then reopen until eight. The first change came in the 1960's with the appearance of American-style department stores, El Corte Inglés and Galerías Preciados, which remained open during the lunch hour. Sunday shopping began in 1986, and in the last couple of years a number of 7–Eleven stores have opened, bringing twenty-four-hour-a-day shopping to Madrid.

Not all traditions are being abandoned. Spaniards remain devoted to *tapas*. These are small portions of food that are available in any Spanish bar and are eaten as snacks before lunch or dinner. Since these two meals are eaten very late—lunch never before two and usually closer to three; dinner sometime after nine—between-meal snacking is understandable and even necessary.

Foods from all over the world, like hot dogs (perritos calientes), are now available in Spain.   Sergio Purtell

However, *tapas* are not snacks like potato chips or pretzels. They are prepared dishes that use ingredients typical in Spanish cooking. Some can be very elaborate. Here are two examples:

Marinated Mushrooms

Heat 2 tablespoons of olive oil in a small, deep casserole. Add 3 tablespoons minced onion and 1 clove minced garlic, and sauté until the onion is wilted. Stir in 1 tablespoon of tomato sauce, 1/4 cup dry white wine, 1/4 cup water, 2 cloves, 1/8 teaspoon saffron, salt, and pepper. Simmer, covered, for 45 minutes, adding more water if necessary. Add 1/2 pound very small mushrooms, cleaned with the stems removed, to the cooking liquid and simmer 5 minutes more. Turn off the heat, cover, and let sit until cool. Refrigerate overnight. Serve cold or at room temperature.

Octopus with Red Peppers and Potatoes

Boil 1 pound of octopus and reserve the liquid. Use 1 cup of the liquid to boil a 1/2 pound of potatoes cut into 1/2-inch cubes; cover and cook until tender. Remove the loose skin from the octopus and cut the tentacles into 1-inch pieces. In an ovenproof casserole heat the oil, add 1 skinned and chopped red pepper, 1 chopped medium onion, and 8 cloves of garlic, and cook slowly until the onion is tender. Add the octopus and sauté for a minute or two. Stir in 1 teaspoon of paprika, 1 bay leaf, and the potatoes. Add 3/4 cup of the liquid in which the potatoes have cooked, salt to taste, bring to a boil, then bake, uncovered, at 350° F for 15 minutes.

Television   Perhaps the most potent agent of cultural change has been television. Spaniards got television in 1954, and it reached into the farthest corners of Spanish society long before most Spaniards could afford a set. The government sponsored *teleclubs* in the villages, giving a set to the village, which then made it available for public viewing, usually in the town hall. By the mid-1970's most Spaniards owned TVs, and a decade later these were color sets.

Until the 1980's there were only two channels, both controlled by the government. Then the Basque and Catalonian regional governments set up stations to broadcast in those languages. Finally, in 1989, the Socialist government permitted private networks to function. By 1989 Spaniards had also begun to acquire satellite dishes in large numbers; the dishes provide access to a number of channels broadcasting in English, French, German, and Italian.

The expansion in the number of channels has not done much to raise the quality of the programming. Spaniards' TV diet is not very different from that of Americans. It includes large numbers of movies, game

Prime Time

What do Spaniards watch on television? Here are the listings for the two state networks for a Sunday chosen at random.

	TV 1		TV 2
12:00	Report on Parliament	12:00	Sports: Basketball, Golf, Water Polo, Skiing, Handball
12:30	News		
1:30	Cartoons		
2:00	Music		
3:00	News		
3:35	Cartoons		
4:05	Movie: *Teacher's Pet* (USA, 1957)		
6:10	Children's Game Show		
6:30	Game Show: *Time Is Money*		
		7:00	*The Avengers*
7:35	Warner Brothers Cartoon		
		8:00	*Cheers*
8:30	News	8:30	Documentary
9:00	*Marriage Agency*: Series from France	9:00	*Moonlighting*
9:35	Movie: *Susan Slade* (USA, 1961)		
		9:50	News
		10:05	Series: *Central Brigade*
		11:00	Sports: Soccer Today
11:40	News		
11:45	Documentary: *Velázquez*		
		12:05	Movie: *Boomerang* (USA, 1947)
12:45	Flamenco Music and Dance		

shows, lots of sports, sitcoms, drama series and soap operas. Many of the series, such as *Dallas* and *Moonlighting*, come from the United States, but a recent big hit was a Venezuelan soap opera called *Cristal*. One thing North Americans would find strange is a much more open attitude to sex, with bare breasts and condom ads quite common.

Television can have an important effect on daily habits. When morning television began in 1986, *Falcon Crest* was put on at 11 A.M. Shopkeepers said that they knew when that series was on because there were far fewer housewives in the stores than there normally would have been at that hour.

Of course, television has not changed everything. The scheduling of programs is very different from that in North America because it has had to accommodate itself to Spanish habits. Prime time is divided, as is the workday. The first part of prime time comes in the long midday break, from two to four or five, formerly the time for the *siesta*. The second part comes at suppertime, between nine and eleven at night.

Ecology

Perhaps because Spaniards are more recent arrivals to the world of consumerism than are North Americans, they have been slower to question some of the less beneficial effects of the consumer culture.

Pollution is a major problem in the cities, in large part because of the growing number of cars. Lead-free gasoline became available only in 1990. In 1989 Spain was charged with 57 infractions of EC environmental regulations, more than any other member state. One of these was for the ongoing destruction of the rare wetlands ecosystem in the Doñana National Park, in the province of Huelva.

Spain has no ecological or "Green" movement of any significance, but ecological consciousness is growing. A poll published in October

1990 found that 86 percent of the respondents felt that pollution was a serious or very serious problem in Spain, up from 55 percent in 1974. It also found that only 19 percent felt that the government was dealing effectively with the problem, compared to 59 percent who felt satisfied in 1974.

One reason for this increased concern was an accident that took place at the Vandellós nuclear power station, near Tarragona, in October 1989, the worst nuclear accident since the 1986 Chernobyl disaster in the Soviet Union. The plant was later closed by the government and will soon be dismantled.

Even so, Spaniards do not seem prepared to make any changes in their style of life to deal with environmental problems. There actually has been a decline in the percentage of people willing to accept special taxes on cars and gasoline to create an environment protection fund.

The Welfare State

Spain today is a welfare state, that is, a state that provides a wide range of social services to its citizens as a matter of right. These services include such things as unemployment insurance, old-age pensions, socialized health care, and education. Curiously, this welfare state was the creation of the Franco dictatorship, although subsequent democratic governments have extended it.

No part of this welfare state touches more Spaniards more frequently than does the school system. The public-school system has grown rapidly since the 1960's, although private schools, almost all of which are run by the Catholic Church, are still widespread. About one third of all elementary and high school students still go to private schools.

College education has become much more accessible as well. In

1960 only 2 percent of eighteen- to twenty-five-year-olds attended a university; by 1980 17 percent did so. More students from humble backgrounds were able to attend. In 1980 40 percent of all university students had parents who had not gone beyond the equivalent of sixth grade.

Spanish Women Today

The extension of schooling has also meant greater opportunities for women. Over half—about 54 percent—of high school students are women. Women also make up just under half of the university students, and they are now a majority not only in such traditionally "female" areas as humanities, but also in economics and law.

Since 1970 women have joined the work force in increasing numbers. On average they still earn considerably less than do men, but that is the case throughout the western world.

During the 1980's more women came to occupy positions of responsibility. One woman held a cabinet post in 1980 and two sat in Felipe González's cabinet. Overall, women make up 13 percent of all members of the national parliament, 6 percent of all members of the regional parliaments, and 3 percent of all mayors. At its 1988 congress the Socialist Party, which has governed Spain since 1982, voted to reserve one quarter of all places on party committees and candidate lists for women.

The Problems of Youth

The changes that have taken place in Spain have meant that the generation born since 1960 has, in many ways, been the most privileged in the country's history. Yet the very speed and extent of the changes, combined with the economic recession that began in the mid-1970's, left Spanish youth confused. Despite general prosperity and greater educational opportunities, it has not necessarily been easy to be young in Spain in recent years.

The relationship between young people and their elders has changed radically. The Spanish language has two different ways for saying "you": one formal to indicate respect, the other informal to indicate familiarity. Into the 1960's children used the formal form when speaking to their parents or teachers. By the 1980's they were using the informal and, in the case of teachers, often using nicknames to their faces.

Drugs have become a significant problem. The use of "soft" drugs like marijuana is widespread, but hard drugs have also become increasingly popular. Alcohol consumption is also very common among the young, but because Spaniards have a much less critical attitude toward alcohol than do North Americans, it is considered less of a problem there. Almost all Spanish cities have a street or square lined with bars catering to the young, with the customers on the sidewalks, or even in the street itself, drink in hand. It is also not uncommon to see young people walking about taking swigs from *litronas*, third-of-a-gallon bottles, of beer.

The starkest expression of the problems of youth was the rise in the late 1970's of *pasotismo*. The name came from the expression "to pass" in a card game and can be translated as "don't give a damn-ism." *Pasotas* took drugs and affected provocative hairstyles and clothing, usually those of the punks. Unlike hippies, or even punks, *pasotas* did not offer a criticism of society; they simply dropped out altogether. Such young people were still around at the end of the 1980's, but they appeared to be fewer in number. Perhaps this is due to an improving economy; perhaps a younger generation, who were born into an already changed country, feels more at home there.

Living Change:
The Voices of Three Generations

The true force of change can best be seen in the lives of individuals and individual families. Of course, no family can ever be "typical" of an entire country, but there are families that embody many of the most important changes that Spain has experienced in recent decades. The Palacios are such a family.

Rufino Palacios was born in 1914 in a small village in the province of Salamanca, near the border with Portugal. His parents were poor farmers and he had only a primary education. He was drafted into Franco's army during the Civil War and rose to master sergeant. He stayed in the army when the war ended and later transferred to the Civil Guard. He then left the force and went to live in his wife's village, a few miles away from his own. Rufino and his wife, Agueda Honorato, have been outside Spain only once, even though the Portuguese border is very close to where they live.

They had three children, a boy born in 1945 and two girls, born in 1948 and 1950. After attending the one-room village school all three went to a private Church school in the nearest big town, Ciudad Rodrigo. The boy, Agustín, would probably have gone to college anyway, but the two girls were fortunate enough to finish school in the late 1960's, just as the universities were opening up, and they both received the benefits. One teaches elementary school in a suburb of Madrid; the other married a Canadian and lives in Toronto, where she teaches French.

Agustín studied medicine. After finishing his training, he worked for a while in a small village and then went into hospital administration. He is now assistant director of the main provincial hospital in Salamanca. In 1975 he married Vicenta Cuesta, the daughter of a schoolteacher of Republican sympathies who had been purged after the Civil

War. She is a high school guidance counselor. They live in a luxurious apartment in the medieval heart of Salamanca, drive an expensive imported car, and take frequent trips abroad.

Their daughter, Alba, was born in 1976. She has lived all her life in a prosperous and democratic Spain. She has attended only public schools and assumes that university education is her right. She also assumes that being a woman will not be an obstacle to choosing the career she wants. She has taken foreign vacations with her parents, in Portugal, Morocco, and England, and one summer she spent a month in a residential language program in England. In 1989–1990 she was in the eighth grade in a junior high school in Toronto, Canada, where her aunt lives.

Uniformity or Diversity?

Who then are the Spaniards? This is a difficult question to answer, for there is a paradox at the heart of the recent Spanish experience.

Over the last twenty years or so Spaniards have been coming to terms with and recognizing their own internal diversity. This can be seen in the Constitution, which enshrines the principles of regional autonomy and linguistic diversity as well as of freedom of religion. It can also be seen in symbolic acts that comment on the intolerance of the past. The most important of these came in June 1990 with the award of the Prince of Asturias Prize for Harmony, a kind of Spanish version of the Nobel Peace Prize, to the Sephardic Jewish communities of the world. The award called the Sephardim an "itinerant Spain that has preserved the linguistic and cultural heritage of its ancestors" and announced that it would "open to them forever the doors of their former homeland."

But then there is the paradox. Spaniards are coming to terms with their historical and actual diversity at the very moment when their own lives are more alike than they have ever been. This is also a moment in which life in Spain is more like that abroad, in western Europe and North America, than ever before and one in which powerful forces will almost certainly carry the process of international homogenization even further in the future.

Under these circumstances, what does it mean to be Spanish? The answer is that the meaning of "Spanishness," or of any national identity, changes over time. There is no unchanging essence that has been shared by all Spaniards across the many centuries of their history, or that they will continue to share in the future.

There has always been diversity, sometimes in religion, sometimes in culture, sometimes in politics. There have been moments of uniformity, but that uniformity has always been imposed and maintained through coercion, by the Inquisition or by the Franco dictatorship. It was not a condition that emerged naturally or could be sustained without force.

This persistent diversity means that stereotypes, at best, draw on a partial picture of Spain and the Spaniards. The images so familiar outside Spain, and especially in the English-speaking world—the Black Legend and "romantic" Spain—are based on single moments of the country's long history or focus on the culture of only one of its various regions. They do not, and cannot, sum up the land and people of Spain, as such stereotypes can never sum up any land or any people.

Bibliography

The best types of books for getting a "feel" for a country are travelers' accounts. There are vast numbers of these for almost all periods of Spain's history. Among the best are George Borrow, *The Bible in Spain* (London, 1843); Richard Ford, *Handbook for Travellers in Spain* (London, 1845); William Dean Howells, *Familiar Spanish Travels* (New York, 1913); James Michener, *Iberia* (New York, 1968); and Laurie Lee, *As I Walked Out One Midsummer's Morning* (New York, 1985). Lee's book has also been made into a television movie.

For entertaining attempts to deal with Spanish "national character" see Fernando Díaz-Plaja, *The Spaniard and the Seven Deadly Sins* (New York, 1967) and Bartolomé Bennassar, *The Spanish Character*, (Berkeley, California, 1979).

There are a few good general histories of Spain: Richard Herr, *Spain* (Englewood Cliffs, New Jersey, 1971); Stanley Payne, *A History of Spain and Portugal* (Madison, Wisconsin, 1973); and Jaime Vicens Vives, *Approaches to the History of Spain* (Berkeley, California, 1967) are the most valuable. The most original introduction to Spanish history remains Gerald Brenan, *The Spanish Labyrinth* (Cambridge, England, 1960). For economics see Jaime Vicens Vives, *An Economic History of Spain* (Princeton, New Jersey, 1969).

For the medieval period the best general books are Gabriel Jackson, *The Making of Medieval Spain* (New York, 1972) and J. F. O'Callaghan, *A History of Medieval Spain* (Ithaca, New York, 1975). On the "Golden Age" see J. H. Elliott, *Imperial Spain* (Harmondsworth, England, 1970) and Henry Kamen, Spain, 1469–1714 (London, 1983).

For the modern period, after 1800, the best general work is Raymond Carr, *Spain, 1808–1975* (New York, 1982).

Chapter I

Charles Gibson, editor, *The Black Legend* (New York, 1971)
    An interesting collection of texts on the Black Legend
William Maltby, *The Black Legend in England* (Durham, North Carolina, 1971)

Chapter II

W. Fisher and H. Bowen-Jones, *Spain: An Introductory Geography* (New York, 1966)

Chapter III

R. J. Harrison, *Spain at the Dawn of History* (London, 1988)
S. J. Keay, *Roman Spain* (Berkeley, California, 1988)
    An up-to-date and comprehensive survey of Spain under the Romans
E. A. Thompson, *The Goths in Spain* (Oxford, England, 1989)
    The best general study of the Visigoths

Chapter IV

Roger Collins, *Early Medieval Spain, 400–1000* (London, 1983) and *The Arab Conquest of Spain* (Oxford, England, 1989)
Derek Lomax, *The Reconquest of Spain* (London, 1978)
    A thorough survey of the Reconquest

Chapter V

Yitzhak Baer, *History of the Jews in Christian Spain* (Philadelphia, 1961)
    A classic account in two volumes
Titus Burckhardt, *Moorish Culture in Spain* (London, 1972)
    A well-illustrated survey
Anwar G. Chejne, *Muslim Spain: Its History and Culture* (Minneapolis, Minnesota, 1974)
Richard Fletcher, *The Quest for El Cid* (London, 1989)
    A study of the mythology that has been built up around the great medieval warrior

Chapter VI

F. Fernandez-Armesto, *Ferdinand and Isabella* (London, 1975)
    An interesting, recent biography of the Catholic Kings
Samuel Eliot Morrison, *Admiral of the Ocean Sea* (Boston, 1942)
    The classic biography of Columbus in three volumes
J. H. Parry, *The Spanish Seaborne Empire* (New York, 1966)
    The best survey of the Spanish overseas empire

Chapters VII and VIII

Marcel Defourneaux, *Daily Life in Spain in the Golden Age* (London, 1970)
    An entertaining look at a wide range of topics
Geoffrey Parker, *Philip II of Spain* (London, 1979) and Peter Pierson, *Philip II* (London, 1975)
    Two good biographies of the great ruler

Chapter IX

Richard Herr, *The Eighteenth Century Revolution in Spain* (Princeton, New Jersey, 1958)
    A superb analysis of enlightened reform in Spain

John Lynch, *Bourbon Spain* (Oxford, England, 1989)
    A good overview of the eighteenth century

Chapter X

William J. Callahan, *Church, Politics and Society in Spain, 1750–1875* (Cambridge, Massachusetts, 1984)
   A superb study of the changing place of the Catholic Church in modern Spanish life
Joseph Harrison, *An Economic History of Modern Spain* (Manchester, England, 1978)
   A good overview
Adrian Shubert, *A Social History of Modern Spain* (Boston, 1990).

Chapter XI

Raymond Carr, *The Spanish Civil War: A History in Pictures* (New York, 1986)
   A wonderfully illustrated volume
Ronald Fraser, *Blood of Spain* (New York, 1979)
   An oral history of the Spanish Civil War
Don Lawson, *The Abraham Lincoln Brigade* (New York, 1989)
George Orwell, *Homage to Catalonia* (Harmondsworth, England, 1966)
   The vivid and thoughtful account of a British participant in the Civil War
Paul Preston, *The Spanish Civil War* (New York, 1986)
   Perhaps the best brief account of the conflict and its complexities

Chapter XII

Raymond Carr and Juan Pablo Fusi, *Spain: Dictatorship to Democracy* (London, 1979)
   A good survey of Spain during the Franco years
Juan Pablo Fusi, *Franco* (New York, 1987)
   The best biography of the Spanish dictator

Chapter XIII

John Hooper, *The Spaniards* (Harmondsworth, England, 1987)
   Entertaining look at Spain in the 1980's by a British journalist

Filmography

Some of the most interesting films about Spanish life have been made by anthropologist Jerome Mintz of Indiana University. These include *Romeria: Day of the Virgin*; *Town Carnival*; and *Perico the Shoemaker*.

The series *Museum Without Walls* includes videos on Goya; Picasso: War, Peace, Love; and the Cubist Epoch. They are available from Kartes Video Communications, Indianapolis.

The Good Fight is a moving exploration of why ordinary American men and women went to fight for the Republic during the Spanish Civil War. The story of the Canadians who fought in Spain is told in *Los Canadienses* by the National Film Board of Canada.

Discography

A number of aspects of Spanish history are covered in audiocassettes available from Gould Media in Mount Vernon, New York: *Spain 1000–1500*; *Spain, 1494–1659*; *Charles V*; *The Spanish Empire*; and *The Spanish Civil War*. All cassettes have been made by leading historians. The same company has the following slide kits about modern Spain: *The Spanish Civil War* and *Spain Under Franco*.

Acknowledgments

Chapter I

Las Casas excerpt on page 5 is from W. S. Maltby, *The Black Legend in England* (Durham, NC: Duke University Press, 1971).

The excerpt on page 5 from John J. Ingalls, *America's War for Humanity,* is cited in Charles Gibson, ed., *The Black Legend* (New York: Alfred A. Knopf, 1972).

The Washington Irving excerpt on page 8 is from P. Irving, *Life and Letters of Washington Irving* (New York: Putnam, 1863).

Excerpt from Prosper Mérimée on page 8 is from his *Carmen,* translated by Lady Mary Loyd (New York: P.F. Collier and Son, 1901).

Excerpts on page 9 are from Harry A. Franck, *Four Months Afoot in Spain* (Garden City, NY: 1926) and G. W. Thornbury, *Life in Spain: Past and Present* (London: Smith, 1859).

Excerpts on pages 11–12 are from Americo Castro, *The Structure of Spanish History* (Princeton: Princeton University Press, 1954) and Claudio Sánchez Albornoz, *España: un enigmo historico* (Buenos Aires: Editorial Sudamericana, 1957).

Chapter II

Excerpt on page 16 is from Rose Macaulay, *Fabled Shore* (Oxford: Oxford University Press, 1986).

The poem on page 17 is from Antonio Machado, translated by Willis Barnstone, *Eighty Poems of Antonio Machado* (New York: Las Americas Publishers, 1959).

Chapter III

The excerpt on page 31 is from Strabo, translated by H. L. Jones, *The Geography of Strabo* (Cambridge, MA: Harvard University Press, 1960).

The excerpt on pages 36–37 is from Appian's *Roman History* (Cambridge, MA: Harvard University Press, 1958).

The excerpt from *Etymologies* on page 43 is in Roger Collins, *Early Medieval Spain* (London: MacMillan, 1983).

The excerpt on King Reccared on page 43 is from Isidore of Seville, translated by G. Dononi and G. B. Ford, *History of the Goths, Vandals and Suevi* (Leiden: E.J. Brill, 1970).

The excerpt on page 44 is from E.A. Thompson, *The Goths in Spain* (Oxford: Oxford University Press, 1969). Reprinted by permission of the publisher.

Chapter IV

The quote on page 47 by Abd al-Rahman is in Jan Read, *The Moors in Spain and Portugal* (Totowa, NJ: Rowman and Littlefield, 1975).

The quote on page 48 by Al-Hakam I is in Titus Burckhardt, *Moorish Culture in Spain* (London: Unwin Hyman, 1972). Reproduced by kind permission of Unwin Hyman Ltd.

The excerpt on page 51 from Ibn Hayyan is cited in Roger Collins, *Early Medieval Spain.*

Map of the Reconquest on page 53 is from Derek Lomax, *The Reconquest of Spain.* Redrawn with the permission of the author.

The excerpt on page 55 is from *Poem of the Cid*, translated by Rita Hamilton and Janet Perry, (London: Penguin, 1984) translation copyright © 1984 by Rita Hamilton.

Chapter V

The excerpt on page 66 is from Moses Maimonides, *The Guide for the Perplexed* (Chicago: University of Chicago Press, 1963). Reprinted by permission of the publisher.

Chapter VI

The excerpt on pages 84–85 is from Francis Bacon, *History of the Reign of King Henry VII* (Indianapolis: Bobbs-Merrill, 1972).

The excerpt on pages 86–87 from Miguel de Cervantes' "The Dogs' Colloquium" is found in John Lynch, *Spain Under the Hapsburgs* (New York: New York University Press, 1981).

The excerpt on pages 88–89 from a poem by Muhammad Rabadan is found in Anwar G. Chejne, *Islam and the West: The Moriscos* (Albany, NY: SUNY Press, 1983). Reprinted by permission of the publisher.

The excerpt on pages 94–95 is from *Journal of Christopher Columbus* translated by

Oliver Duncan and J. E. Kelley, Jr. (Norman, OK: University of Oklahoma Press, 1989).

Chapter VII
The excerpts on pages 105–106 are found in William Prescott, *History of the Reign of Philip II* (Philadelphia: Lippincott, 1874).
The excerpts on the Armada on pages 110 and 111 are from John Rodger Scott Whiting, *Enterprise of England* (New York: St. Martin's Press, 1988). Reprinted by permission of the publisher.
The excerpt on pages 111–112 is from Edward, Earl of Clarendon, *The History of the Rebellion* (Oxford: Clarendon Press, 1888).
The genealogical chart on page 100 is from A. W. Lovett, *Early Hapsburg Spain 1517–1598* (Oxford: Oxford University Press, 1986). Reprinted by permission of the publisher.

Chapter VIII
The excerpt on page 116 is from John Lynch, *Spain Under the Hapsburgs* (New York: New York University Press, 1981).
The excerpt on pages 122–123 is from William Christian, *Local Religion in Sixteenth Century Castile* (Princeton: Princeton University Press, 1981). Reprinted by permission of the publisher.
The excerpt on page 125 from *Lazarillo de Tormes* is from Michael Alpert, translator, *Two Spanish Picaresque Novels* (Harmondsworth: Penguin Classics, 1969). Copyright © 1969 by Michael Alpert. Reprinted by permission of the publisher.
The excerpt on pages 126–127 from *Don Quixote* is from Samuel Putnam, editor and translator, *The Portable Cervantes* (New York: Viking Penguin, 1951). Copyright 1951 by Samuel Putnam, renewed © 1979 by Hilary Putnam. Reprinted by permission of Viking Penguin, a division of Penguin Books USA Inc.

Chapter IX
The excerpt on pages 138–139 is from Joseph Townsend, *A Journey Through Spain in the Years 1786 and 1787* (London: Dilly, 1792).
The excerpt on pages 142–143 is from Alexander von Humboldt, *Political Essay on the Kingdom of New Spain* (New York: Alfred A. Knopf, 1972).

Chapter X
The excerpt on pages 162–163 is from Ángel Ganivet, translated by J.R. Carey, *Spain: An Interpretation* (London: Eyre and Spottiswoods, 1946).
The excerpt on pages 164–165 is from Dolores Ibarruri, *They Shall Not Pass* (New York: International Publishers, 1966).

Chapter XI
"The Importance of Agrarian Reform" on page 174 from Jerome Mintz, *The*

· 236 ·

Anarchists of Casas Viejas (Chicago: University of Chicago Press, 1982). Reprinted by permission of the publisher.

The excerpt on page 178 is from George Orwell, *Homage to Catalonia* (New York: Harcourt Brace Jovanovich, Inc., 1969). Copyright 1952 and renewed 1980 by Sonia Brownell Orwell. Reprinted by permission of the publisher.

The Fraser Lawton letters on pages 178–179 courtesy of Mr. Jack Goering, Port Credit, Ontario.

"Dawn" on pages 192–193 is by Federico García Lorca from *Poet in New York* (New York: Farrar, Straus and Giroux, Inc., 1988). Translation copyright ©1988 by the Estate of Federico García Lorca, and Greg Simon and Steven F. White. Reprinted by permission of the publisher.

Chapter XII

Excerpts on pages 203 and 205 are from Carmen Martín Gaite, *Usos amorosos de la postguerra española* (Barcelona: Anagrama, 1987).

Chapter XIII

Tapas recipes on pages 219–220 are from Penelope Casas, *Tapas: The Little Dishes of Spain* (New York: Alfred A. Knopf, Inc., 1985). Reprinted by permission of the publisher.

Index

Numbers in *italics* refer to illustrations.

music, 69–72, 73, 185–86, 198, 202, 214, 216

Salamanca, 203, *204*
Sánchez Ferlosio, Raphael, *Jarama*, 197
Sancho I ("the Fat"), King, 49, 51
Sancho II, King, 52
Santander, 14, *14*, 19, 29
Santiago de Compostela, 68, *71*
Sant Jordi, Jordi de, 72
Segovia, 28, 40, 115–16
Segovia, Andrés, 186
Sephardim, 91, 227
Sepúlveda, Juan Ginés de, 1–2
Seville, 20, 56, 57, 118
sharia (Islamic law), 56
ships, 107, *108*, 109, 110–11, 117–18
Silver Age, 185
slavery, 2, 38, 44
socialism, 169, 170, 173, 175, 181, 211, 224
Soria, 28
Spain, names of, 29, 47
Spanish-American War, 5, 158–59, *159*
Spanish Civil War, 12, 146, 168, 176–81, *182*, 183, *183*, 184–85, *185*
Spanish empire, 114–117
Spanish identity, 1, 7, 10, 11–12, 24–25, 54, 227–28
Spanish language, ix, 10, 63, 72, 225
Spanish literature, 155–58
"Spanish ulcer," 151
sports, 210, 214, 215, *215*, 216, 217, *217*, 218
Suarez, President Adolfo, 210, *211*
Suebic dynasty, 39, 41

tableland (*meseta*), 14, 16–17, *18*, 19, 22
Tagus River, 18
taifa kingdoms, 51–52, 54–56
Tarragona, 223
television, 198, 201, 215–16, 217, 220–22
Teresa of Avila, 120, 122
Third Council of Toledo, 43
Thirty Years' War, 113
Titian, portrait of Charles V, *103*
Toledo, 46, 52, 68, 115–16
Torrero, Diego Muñoz, 152
tourism, 200
Trastámara dynasty, 72
trees, 16, 22, 24
troubadors, 72

Turina, Joaquín, 186
Twelve Years' Truce, 109

Ummayad dynasty, 46, 47, 62, 65
Unamuno, Miguel de, 161
    Concerning Traditionalism, 163
    Mist, 191

Valencia, 21, 22, 54, 57, 86, 130
Valladalid, 22
Velázquez, Diego, 125
    The Maids of Honor, 128
    The Surrender of Breda, 128
Verdaguer, Jacinto, 157
Visigothic Spain, 41–44

warfare, 30, 45, 48, 52, 102, 105, 106, 109, 112–13, 146, 148, 151
War of Independence, 145, 146, 151
War of the Spanish Succession, 129, 130
welfare state, 223–24
"wet Spain," 21–22
wine, 21–22, 162
women, 38, 56, 152–53, 164–65, 202–3, 224
workhouses (*hospicios*), 138–39, 140
World War I, 168, 169, 172, 188
World War II, 205

youth, 201–2, 203, *204*, 205, 224–25

Zamora, 28

· 244 ·